The
FORGOTTEN
PAST

An Eclectic Collection of Little
Known Stories from the
Annals of History

Andrew Vinken

Matador
9 Priory Business Park,
Wistow Road, Kibworth Beauchamp,
Leicestershire, LE8 0RX
Tel: 0116 279 2299
Email: books@troubador.co.uk
Web: www.troubador.co.uk/matador
Twitter: @matadorbooks

ISBN 978 1789018 790

British Library Cataloguing in Publication Data.
A catalogue record for this book is available from the British Library.

Typeset in 11pt Adobe Caslon Pro by Troubador Publishing Ltd, Leicester, UK

Matador is an imprint of Troubador Publishing Ltd

Dedicated to the memory of my good friend
Simon James Capey
1963-2013

CONTENTS

INTRODUCTION

I suppose I have always had a keen interest in history, but it was only when studying at undergraduate level that I realised what it was that really excited me about the subject. We've all been taught about kings and queens, great battles and the rise and fall of empires. The term historians have coined for this is **'history from above'**. But what about the ordinary folk? What about almost everybody who ever existed? What about the places where no earth-shattering events have ever occurred? I realised that what interested me most were the people and places that did not make it into the school curriculum. The term historians use for this is **'history from below'**.

Of course, we cannot know everything that has ever happened. In fact, what we do know is but a tiny fraction of everything that has ever happened. Nevertheless, it is the things we do know, but which have been largely forgotten, that this book is about. In what follows, kings and queens and famous places do put in occasional appearances, but do so in secondary roles. The stories I have included in this book are about people and places that, for the most part, do not spring readily to mind but which, partly as a consequence of their obscurity, form fascinating tales nonetheless.

So, if you too have an interest in things over which time has drawn a veil, read on and prepare to discover some history from below. I hope you enjoy the stories.

Andrew Vinken
Buckinghamshire, England
January 2019

ONE

WRIGHT? WRONG!

The day of 26 June 2013 was a monumental one in aviation history. "Why, what happened?", I hear you say. Well, I'll tell you. But in order to do so we need to go back more than 140 years, to 1 January 1874. On this day, in Leutershausen, Bavaria, to Karl and Babetta Weisskopf, was born a boy by the name of Gustave. By the time he reached school age, he had developed a lively interest in flight. He built models that flew, and was even recorded jumping off roofs with homemade wings attached to his arms! Fortunately, he seems to have come to little harm.

Sadly, by 1887 both his parents were dead, and so young Gustave had to make his own way in the world. He trained as a mechanic and eventually found work on a Norwegian ship called *The Gromund*, sailing between Europe and South America.

Sometime during 1893, Weisskopf arrived in the USA and almost immediately anglicised his surname

1

*Gustave
Whitehead*

to Whitehead. He first found work with Harvard University, at their Blue Hill Weather Observatory, where, among other things, his duties included the testing of kites.

In 1896, Whitehead found more gainful employment at the Boston Aeronautical Society, as a mechanic. In this capacity, he built a number of gliders and made a few flights in them himself. Around this time, he also gained an interest in the development of engines, and he eventually built several of his own examples. What followed was perhaps inevitable. Gustave began to work on the unrealised dream of powered flight. He constructed a number of prototypes, until...

On 14 August 1901, Whitehead took his latest attempt at a heavier-than-air aircraft, unimaginatively called 'Number 21', to a site near the village of Fairfield, about 1.5 miles outside Bridgeport, Connecticut. It had a wingspan of 36 feet and was powered by two engines. A 10-horsepower engine provided power to the wheels, to propel the craft to take-off speed, and a 20-horsepower engine powered two propellers for momentum in flight.

*Gustave
Whitehead's
'Number 21'*

The world's press had been invited and, at 5.02am, the contraption started to move along the ground, gathering speed as it went. Then, to the amazement of those in attendance, Whitehead actually took off! His first flight covered a distance of about half a mile, or around 2,600 feet. He then took off again, this time achieving a distance of approximately

one and a half miles, or about 7,800 feet, at a steady height of around 50 feet. This momentous achievement, witnessed by numerous individuals, was front-page news around the world, with more than 130 contemporary newspaper articles reporting the flights.

Compare this, if you will, to the first flight of the Wright brothers' 'Flyer', on 17 December 1903, during which Orville Wright achieved a distance of only 120 feet. Considering that the wingspan of a Boeing 747 is 196 feet, this is a somewhat underwhelming distance!

So, what is the problem? If Whitehead achieved powered flight in a heavier-than-air aircraft in August 1901, why do the history books record Orville Wright's punier effort of December 1903 as the first occasion this feat was accomplished?

The answer seems to be photographic evidence. Sharp-imaged, good-quality photographs exist to prove that the Flyer flew. By comparison, only one very blurred image of Whitehead's achievement was ever known to have existed, and that has since been lost. All that remains today is an even less clear image, included in a photograph taken in 1906 at an Aero Club of America Exhibition, purporting to show the original

The Wright brothers' 'Flyer'

3

photograph as part of the exhibition. Unsurprisingly, a small section of a 1906 photograph depicting a blurred photograph is very blurred indeed, and is therefore inadmissible as evidence.

In later years, while never achieving the level of success enjoyed by the Wright brothers, Whitehead became a leading supplier of engines and airframes. In 1907, a flying machine fitted with a Whitehead engine, the construction of which had been financed by the United States Navy, was displayed at the World Fair in Jamestown, Virginia. Thus the first aircraft in US military history was powered by one of Gustave's engines!

On 10 October 1927, Whitehead was repairing a car and was in the process of attempting to lift out the engine. Sadly, while lifting this heavy weight, he suffered a heart attack. Despite managing to stagger back into his house, the attack proved fatal. Gustave was 53 years old at the time of his death.

To date, two replicas of Whitehead's 'Number 21' have been constructed: one in the USA in 1986, and one in Germany in 1997. Both replicas flew successfully, thereby proving the airworthiness of the original aircraft.

"So, what happened on 26 June 2013?" Well, I was just coming to that. A little earlier that year, *Jane's All the World's Aircraft*, the world's leading authority on aviation history, having weighed the evidence, formally recognised Gustave Whitehead's flight, on 14 August 1901, as the first manned flight of a heavier-than-air aircraft. Official recognition followed; and on 26 June, Gustave's achievement was commemorated by an enactment of legislation signed by the Connecticut

State Governor. So, it's official: the first person to take to the skies in a heavier-than-air powered aircraft was Gustave Whitehead and not Orville Wright! How different his life might have been had he hired a decent photographer on that summer's day in 1901.

TWO

THE TRAIN NOW DEPARTING

At the beginning of the nineteenth century, the population of London stood at just under one million. By 1851, it had swollen to almost two and a half million. Increased mechanisation meant less work for agricultural labourers, but also more work in newly built factories in towns and cities across the UK. Consequently, the predominantly rural population of the eighteenth century rapidly migrated to urban areas to find work. This meant that, by the middle of the nineteenth century, London had become a very crowded place indeed.

Understandably, there were problems accommodating such a rapidly increasing population, and overcrowding was a serious issue. But it was not only the living that were running out of room; existing graveyards were literally overflowing with the dead! Traditionally, the deceased had been interred in small churchyards dotted around the city, but by the 1840s the 200 or so graveyards were so congested that graves were being reused with increasing regularity.

Disinterred corpses, or parts thereof, littered churchyards, and fluids and other matter from decomposing cadavers began finding their way into the local water supplies. Needless to say, the city experienced regular outbreaks of diseases such as cholera and typhoid. Between 1848 and 1849, a serious cholera epidemic killed more than 14,500 people, merely compounding the problem of the overcrowded graveyards. The unburied dead were killing the living, and in so doing further increased the demand for burial space.

Something had to be done. A ring of new large cemeteries, outside of London's urban area, was proposed and duly adopted by the authorities. Kensal Green Cemetery, to the west of London, and Highgate Cemetery to the north, are two well-known examples. These cemeteries were intended for the burial of all of London's deceased, regardless of wealth or social standing. Nevertheless, the size of one's plot and monument soon became a status symbol for well-to-do Londoners.

The famous Victorian engineer, Isambard Kingdom Brunel, is buried at Kensal Green, and Karl Marx, author of *The Communist Manifesto*, is interred at Highgate. Kensal Green Cemetery has even been immortalised in poetry. G. K. Chesterton's poem, *The Rolling English Road*, contains the lines: "For there is good news yet to hear and fine things to be seen; Before we go to Paradise by way of Kensal Green." Although, by the time of his death, Chesterton was living in

*G. K.
Chesterton*

Beaconsfield, Buckinghamshire, and so was not himself laid to rest at Kensal Green.

However, as London's population continued to grow, the urban area expanded proportionally, and it became apparent that even these new cemeteries would soon be engulfed by the sprawl of the city's suburbs. A more radical solution would be required. Enter Sir Richard Broun, an entrepreneur and eccentric. Broun proposed the purchase of a 2,000-acre plot of land 23 miles (37km) to the south-west of London, at Brookwood in Surrey, to serve as a super-cemetery for the dead of the city.

Brookwood Cemetery would be far enough from the expanding metropolis that it would neither present a health hazard nor be enveloped by future burgeoning developments. Additionally, the price of the land at Brookwood was considerably cheaper than similar-sized plots closer to the city, meaning more affordable burials for London's less well-off. The only remaining problem was how to get the deceased individual, plus his or her grieving friends and relatives, to the graveside.

Once again, Broun was the man. He proposed the construction of a small branch line off the London to Southampton railway. Special trains could thus take the departed and mourners alike from London's Waterloo Station directly to the cemetery. Despite reservations among the more conservative about using the new-fangled, noisy, smelly and irreverent trains for such a purpose, an Act of Parliament was passed, in June

1852, creating the London Necropolis & National Mausoleum Company – later shortened to the London Necropolis Company.

The rail operator, London and South Western Railway, was concerned that existing passengers might be put off using its services if they discovered that they were

Interesting company logo

sharing trains with the dead. Consequently, it was decided that Necropolis trains would need to be run on an entirely separate timetable, using dedicated rolling stock. Work was undertaken, a timetable drawn up and, on 7 November 1854, the grounds of Brookwood Cemetery were consecrated. Six days later, the first regular funeral train the world had ever seen was itself ready to depart.

Mourners travelled in first-, second- or third-class compartments, depending on their means – and, bizarrely, so did the deceased. One would have thought that the degree of comfort and the social standing of the company would have been of little consequence once you were dead, yet it seems that the British class system extended even beyond the mortal coil!

Another unusual consequence of the regular funeral train concerned the golf course that was located next to the cemetery. London-based golfers quickly realised that 'the stiffs' express', as it soon became known, was the fastest and most convenient way of getting to and from the course. As a result, golfers dressed in mourning wear, and purporting to be acquainted with

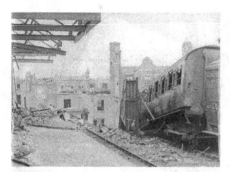

*The damaged
terminus of
the London
Necropolis
Company*

the departed, frequently made use of the service. Quite what excuse they gave for the presence of their golf clubs has unfortunately been lost in the mists of time!

After an encouraging start, things did not go as well as planned for the London Necropolis Company. With the legalisation of cremation in the UK in 1885, the need for burial space declined steadily. As the popularity of cremation grew, so the demand for inhumations fell away. During 87 years of operation, just over 200,000 burials were conducted at Brookwood Cemetery, equating to around 2,300 per year.

The terminus of the London Necropolis Company at Waterloo Station was badly damaged during an air raid by Germany's Luftwaffe on 16 April 1941 and was never used again. Although occasional services continued to run from the main terminus at Waterloo, demand was by then so low that the London Necropolis Company soon ceased operations entirely. The deceased may not have been in need of their services anymore, but I expect the golfers were devastated!

THREE

THE PRINCE OF POYAIS

In the twenty-first century, with the internet age now in its fourth decade, we have become used to scams and cons perpetrated by the unseen. Emails promising magnificent returns on modest investments extort money from the vulnerable, or account details are obtained by the implication that security has been compromised. Even before internet fraud was such big business, con artists have long swindled the unsuspecting through such scams as the issue of worthless stocks and bonds. However, there is one swindler who stands head and shoulders above the rest. I give you Gregor MacGregor, the man who invented an entirely fictitious country for monetary gain!

Gregor MacGregor was born on Christmas Eve 1786 in Stirlingshire, Scotland. The MacGregor clan was firmly embedded in the history of the Highlands: his great-great-uncle was none other than Rob Roy of Jacobite Rising fame. Gregor joined the British Army

*Gregor
MacGregor
(1786–1845)*

in 1803 at the tender age of 16, but by 1810 had resigned following a disagreement with a superior officer. Not long after this, the Venezuelan revolutionary, General Francisco de Miranda, visited London, and was well received owing to his ongoing struggles against one of Britain's main adversaries: the Spanish. Spotting an opportunity to make use of his military training, and no doubt with notions of glorious victories ahead, Gregor departed for Venezuela, arriving in April 1812.

Once there, MacGregor approached General de Miranda directly, and was immediately appointed to the rank of colonel. He also ingratiated himself with another revolutionary leader, Simon Bolivar, by marrying his cousin, Dona Josefa Antonia Andrea Aristeguieta y Lovera. Mercifully, she was thereafter known by her married name of Josefa MacGregor!

The subsequent military career of Gregor MacGregor was patchy, to say the least. He fought against the Spanish, on behalf of Venezuela and neighbouring New Granada, with limited success. His defeats significantly outnumbered his victories, and his most celebrated accomplishment was actually a tactical retreat. Nevertheless, he remained well respected in certain Central and South American communities, although he had, by 1819, fallen foul of his relative by marriage, Simon Bolivar, who threatened to have him hanged if he ever caught up with him! Perhaps mindful of this, MacGregor next appeared at Cape Gracias a Dios on the Gulf of Honduras, having put some

*Francisco
de Miranda
(1750–1816)*

considerable distance between himself and the disgruntled Bolivar.

Here he presented himself to the court of King George Frederic Augustus of the Mosquito Coast. The title was grand, but the 'King' was in effect a tribal chieftain with relatively little control over the country he was attempting to rule. Notwithstanding his shaky sovereignty, on 29 April 1820, King George granted MacGregor 12,500 square miles of Mosquito territory in exchange for jewellery and rum. The land in question was not suitable for cultivation and was incapable of sustaining livestock. There

*Simon Bolivar
(1783–1830)*

had once been a small settlement along the coast but this had been long abandoned. By 1820, all that was visible was a small overgrown graveyard. The area granted to MacGregor is to be found in modern-day Honduras and remains undeveloped to this day.

In 1821, MacGregor returned to London, and this is where the story starts to get interesting. He referred to himself as the 'Cazique of Poyais' – both title and country being entirely of his own creation. He claimed that 'Cazique' was a term equivalent to 'Prince' and that it had been bestowed upon him by the Mosquito King. Amazingly, his story was swallowed, hook, line and sinker! He was entertained by the upper echelons of society and was even given an official reception by the Lord Mayor of London.

MacGregor claimed to be in London in order to attend the coronation of King George IV on behalf of the Poyer people, and he even produced a printed proclamation which he stated had been issued to the

Poyers on 13 April 1821. This astonishing document concluded with the words: "I now bid you farewell for a while... I trust that through the kindness of Almighty Providence, I shall be again enabled to return amongst you, and that then it will be my pleasing duty to hail you as affectionate friends, and yours to receive me as your faithful Cazique and Father."

What happened next took things to a whole other level. MacGregor drafted a constitution and commercial and banking systems for Poyais, and even introduced an honours system! He opened Poyasian offices in Edinburgh, Glasgow and London, to sell land certificates and to arrange transport for settlers. He even produced a guidebook of Poyais for would-be settlers that ran to 355 pages! The book described the climate as being agreeable to the European constitution, the soil as fertile, and fish and game as plentiful. He even created a fictional capital city, St Joseph, containing a theatre, opera house, cathedral and wide boulevards, not to mention a population of around 20,000.

In addition to the income from the land certificates, MacGregor also obtained a loan of £200,000 from a London bank, secured on the revenues of the Government of Poyais. This amount in 1821 equates to approximately £15 million today! A further con involved the Bank of Scotland's official printer, whom MacGregor used to have Bank of Poyais dollar notes printed, which he then

Poyais, as depicted in MacGregor's guidebook

exchanged with settlers for pounds sterling or gold. Thus he sold them certificates for non-existent plots of land and then gave them worthless notes in exchange for hard currency or precious metal.

A Bank of Poyais dollar note

Needless to say, once the settlers arrived, they were extremely bemused to find that nothing was as described by MacGregor. Those natives that they managed to encounter knew nothing of Poyais or its Cazique. Conditions were harsh, and yellow fever and malaria swept through the encampment. Tragically, of the approximately 250 who made the journey, as many as 200 died. Certainly, less than 50 ever returned to British shores.

Unsurprisingly, MacGregor left England just before the survivors arrived back in October 1823. Surprisingly, however, this did not stop him from pursuing his scam elsewhere, and even returning to London in 1827 for another try, although he was never again to enjoy the success of his first deception.

That MacGregor managed to evade successful prosecution and imprisonment is, I imagine, testament to his credibility and his ability to simply brazen it out. He never actually conceded that Poyais did not exist.

After the death of Josefa in 1838, MacGregor settled in Venezuela, where he died on 4 December 1845. Astonishingly, he was buried with full military honours in Caracas Cathedral, with the president, cabinet ministers and military chiefs of staff marching behind the coffin. Even after his death he seems to have been able to continue the habit of overstating his achievements. A swindler and a crook no doubt, but you have to hand it to him – he did it on an impressive scale!

FOUR

AMERICA – AMERIGO OR AMERIKE?

If you ask a historian today why the continent of America is so called, the chances are they will tell you that it is named after the Italian explorer Amerigo Vespucci. And they may well be right. There is, however, a lesser-known candidate for the accolade and, although it seems unlikely that documentary evidence will emerge to settle the matter one way or the other, I thought it might be a worthwhile exercise to have a look at the basis of both assertions.

Amerigo Vespucci was born in Florence and spent most of his life as a merchant. However, between 1499 and 1502, he took part in a number of voyages of discovery to what we now know as the east coast of South America, principally as an observer. Two accounts of the expeditions, attributed to Vespucci, were published between 1502 and 1504, and it was through these accounts that the expeditions became

*Amerigo
Vespucci
(1454–1512)*

widely known in Europe. In 1507, Martin Waldseemuller, a German cartographer, produced a world map. On the map he named the new continent 'America', purportedly after Vespucci's first name.

However, there are a couple of potential issues with this contention. Firstly, Vespucci did not command the expeditions, nor did he finance them. He is known as the potential author of accounts of the voyages, but not as a leading player in them. Normal practice would be to name a newly discovered land either in honour of the voyage's commander, as in the Cook Islands, named after Captain James Cook, or after the patron of the expedition.

Secondly, the protocol for the naming of places after people's first names is that it is usually reserved for royalty; think of Jamestown or Charlestown, named after English kings. As first names are shared by many people, place names derived from individuals of more common origin normally refer to the surname of the person in question: Rhodesia, for example, named after Cecil Rhodes, or Bolivia, after Simon Bolivar. While a contemporary source does exist, suggesting that it would be appropriate to name the newly discovered continent after Amerigo Vespucci, Waldseemuller himself seems to have remained enigmatically silent on his choice of the name.

So, if not Vespucci, then who else could be the origin of the name 'America'? Step forward Richard Amerike. Like Vespucci, Amerike was a merchant, although he hailed from the less glamorous port city of Bristol in the west of England. As a merchant, however, he was very successful and, in addition to being wealthy, was also sheriff of Bristol. It is through his association with a voyage undertaken by the Venetian explorer Giovanni Caboto, in 1497, that his claim to fame lies. Giovanni Caboto is better known today by the anglicised version of his name: John Cabot.

Between 1485 and 1490, Cabot travelled extensively and was regarded as a skilful mariner. Believing the world to be round, and aware of valuable spices and other exotic goods produced in the East, he was certain that by sailing west he could reach the Orient from the other direction in a faster time and so exploit the wealth of commodities to be found there.

Consequently, Cabot came to Bristol in 1495 in the hope of finding a sponsor for a voyage of discovery to the West. There, he was introduced to a syndicate of businessmen equally keen on opening up trade with the known lands far to the east. Impressed by Cabot's proposal to head westwards in search of the East, the leader of the syndicate, Richard Amerike, arranged an audience with King Henry VII of England. On 5 March 1496, the King granted Cabot a letter of authority to undertake a voyage and claim lands for the monarch.

John Cabot
(c. 1450–c. 1500)

Cabot was to be provided with a brand-new ship for the voyage, and it is generally accepted that it was Amerike who was the principal financier of the project, and also the source of the oak timbers used in the construction, the trees having been felled on his family estate. In return, Amerike is believed to have requested that any new-found lands be named in his honour. On

19

20 May 1497, *The Matthew*, as it was named, set sail from Bristol with a crew of 18 carefully selected sailors. After a journey of 34 days, sailors of *The Matthew* did indeed sight Newfoundland, and went ashore.

All very good, but what evidence do we have to assert that the newly discovered continent was actually named after Richard Amerike? Well, none it would seem. It is just worth considering a few points before deciding for oneself either way. Firstly, Cabot arrived in Newfoundland in 1497 – at least two years before Vespucci made landfall in South America. Secondly, Amerike is a surname, while Amerigo is a first name. As described above, unless naming somewhere after royalty, it is usual practice to opt for the surname of an individual. Thirdly, and perhaps most interesting of all, is the stars and stripes of the Amerike family coat of arms!

While many assume that the flag of the United States of America was born out of George Washington's family coat of arms, which was also composed of a stars and stripes motif, the Amerike family pre-dated the Washington connection with the continent by almost 300 years. Also, the American Flag Research Center in Massachusetts has confirmed that the heraldic origin of the American flag is not positively known.

Taking each of the points of the Amerike claim on their own, none are particularly convincing. However, when one looks at them cumulatively, a very plausible case does seem to emerge to suggest that, perhaps, on this occasion, popular opinion is wrong.

However, regardless of all the arguments and counter-arguments, there is one undeniable fact that ought to give Vespucci the bragging rights: at least he went there. Amerike never even set foot in the place!

FIVE

WHO KILLED
SIR EDMUND GODFREY?

On 17 October 1678, Sir Edmund Godfrey was discovered lying face down in a ditch on Primrose Hill, in north-west London. He had been strangled and his neck broken. He had also been run through with his own sword. The perpetrator, or perpetrators, had clearly adopted a 'belt and braces' approach to the killing. But who had murdered the prominent merchant and Justice of the Peace, and why?

A decent enough chap by all accounts, Godfrey had been knighted in 1666 for services rendered during the Great Plague of 1665, when he had remained at his post in London while many others fled to the countryside in the hope of avoiding infection. He was an Anglican by religion – meaning that he leaned towards the Protestant theology of the Church of England – although he maintained a number of Catholic acquaintances. On the face of it,

*Sir Edmund
Godfrey*

Sir Edmund Godfrey seemed like an all-round good egg.

His money and rings were still about his person when his body was discovered, so it was clear that robbery was not the motive behind the killing. But why would anybody want him dead? Well, it would appear that all was not quite as it seemed.

On 1 June 1670, King Charles II of England and King Louis XIV of France signed a treaty, known as the 'Secret Treaty of Dover'. Basically, the treaty entailed the English King and country reverting back to Catholicism in return for monetary gain. As is generally the way with these things, the secret treaty did not remain secret for very long, and many prominent individuals who were opposed to the country's re-alliance with the Roman Catholic Church began to hatch a plot to replace the King with a republic. The plotters were led by Sir Robert Peyton, a Member of Parliament, and the 'Peyton Gang', as they became known, included our man Godfrey.

A further complication concerns an individual by the name of Titus Oates, and a plan known as 'The Popish Plot'. Irrespective of the secret treaty, King Charles II was still Protestant, whereas his brother James was Catholic. Oates claimed to have uncovered evidence of a plot by prominent Catholics to assassinate the King and so bring his Catholic brother to the throne of England. No such plan existed, and the plot was a complete fabrication on the part of Oates. As a Justice of the Peace, Sir Edmund Godfrey had been approached by Oates and his conspirator, Israel Tonge, and asked to take their oaths that the evidence that they presented was true. Godfrey, diligent but perhaps somewhat naive, demanded to see documentary corroboration of the plot and, when this was provided, they duly took their depositions on 28 September 1678.

After the discovery of Godfrey's body, Oates immediately claimed that the murder had been the work of Catholic plotters, and a certain William Bedloe,

*Titus Oates
(1649–1705)*

another of Oates's accomplices, maintained that he had been killed in order to steal his papers relating to the depositions. Given that both witnesses were still alive and well, this seems a most improbable motive, as Oates and Tonge would only have needed to repeat their oaths before another magistrate. When Bedloe named John Belasyse, 1st Baron Belasyse, as the man behind the deed, even the King was unable to take the matter seriously. Apparently, Belasyse was so gout ridden that he was hardly able to stand!

Nevertheless, two months after the murder, another Catholic, Miles Prance, was accused of involvement in the death. He was arrested and tortured. Unsurprisingly, during torture he confessed to being aware of a plan to kill Godfrey, although he denied any direct connection with the murder. Instead, he named three men from the lower echelons of society as the perpetrators. They were Robert Green, Henry Berry and Lawrence Hill. Being unable to afford much in the way of legal representation, they were tried and quickly convicted of the murder. On 5 February 1679, all three were hanged on Primrose Hill, where the body had been discovered. The English are known today for having a slightly dark sense of humour, and it was no different back in the late seventeenth century. Primrose Hill quickly became known as 'Greenberry Hill', after the surnames of the executed men, and it was many decades before the original name returned to prominence.

Even before the hangings, Prance had recanted his confession. However, on being sent back to prison, he quickly recanted his original recantation, and so the men were hastily dispatched before he could change his mind again. It later transpired that Prance's evidence, obtained under extreme duress, was false; and when he was accused of perjury, he confessed. Thus the murder of Edmund Godfrey remains unsolved to this day.

At a distance of almost three and a half centuries, all we are left with today are theories. Was Godfrey killed by Catholics, concerned that he might have incriminating evidence against them, or by Protestants because of his Catholic associations? Could he have been bumped off by Oates or his conspirators because he knew their claims were nothing but a tissue of lies? Perhaps he was done in by Oates' cronies, simply so they could blame it on the Catholics and so give credence to the idea of a Popish Plot. There was even a claim, made in 1687, that Godfrey had committed suicide. Quite how you strangle yourself, break your own neck and then run yourself through with a sword post-mortem was not elaborated upon. If, however, they had meant that someone wanted to make his suicide look like murder, then presumably we are back to Oates and a variant on the 'blame the Catholics' theory.

Two investigations undertaken during the twentieth century both concluded that it was unlikely that Godfrey was killed for any of the reasons stated above. He was, after all, a magistrate, and it was deemed more likely that he was murdered by someone who had a grudge against him for having been hauled into court. The chief suspect based on this theory was Philip Herbert, 7th Earl of Pembroke, who sometime earlier had been prosecuted for murder by Godfrey.

All in all, it is beginning to look as though it would have been an easier task to draw up a list of the people who did not have a motive for killing poor old Sir Edmund Godfrey. Whoever did the deed could well have been standing at the front of a rather long queue!

SIX

WAS KING ARTHUR
PART ITALIAN?

Most of us will be familiar with the legend of King
Arthur and the sword in the stone. According to the
story, the hilt of a sword named 'Excalibur' protruded
from a large stone, and only the true King of England
would be able to pull the sword from the stone. Arthur,
it turned out, was the man, and he proceeded to extract
the sword as easily as if he were drawing it from a
scabbard. It is said that he went on to defend England
against Saxon invaders during the fifth and sixth
centuries CE. Whether the man ever actually existed
is much debated, and the legend that comes down to
us today dates from the twelfth century CE, the best-
known source being Geoffrey of Monmouth's *Historia
Regum Britanniae* (*History of the Kings of Britain*).

As you can imagine, swords encased in stone do
not crop up very often in history; and so, when one
hears about another one, eyebrows are raised. However,

in this second example, not only do we have biographical information about the man behind the story, but the sword in the stone is still in existence.

San Galgano was born in Chiusdino, in the modern-day Italian province of Siena, in 1148. Being of noble descent, he trained as a knight; but far from being chivalrous, he was regarded by contemporaries as violent and arrogant. His personality took a turn for the better, however, following a vision of the Archangel Michael, who supposedly revealed to San Galgano the route to salvation. Thereafter, he announced that he was to become a hermit and, further, that he would be taking up residence in a nearby cave. But before doing so, he decided to pay one last visit to his fiancée, although he never actually made it that far. On his way there, his horse reared up and he was thrown off it. He needn't have worried, however, because an invisible force lifted him to his feet, and a heavenly voice directed him to a hill called 'Montesiepi', where he supposedly saw a vision of a round temple with Mary, Jesus and the Twelve Apostles in attendance.

A later depiction of King Arthur and Excalibur

The voice instructed him to climb the hill, and upon him reaching the top it spoke again, demanding that he renounce all his worldly desires. San Galgano, by now having quite a bad day, objected to this, saying it would be equally easy to split a stone with a sword. To make his point, he drew his sword and thrust it at a large stone. To his astonishment, the sword passed straight into the stone, and has been firmly stuck there ever since. San Galgano immediately got the message, and thereafter lived as a hermit on Montesiepi. After

An enigmatic artefact if ever there was one!

his death, a round chapel was built on top of the hill, incorporating the sword in the stone.

A nice story, but complete hogwash, I'm sure you'll agree. Well, hogwash almost certainly, but it's just that there are a couple of things that might cause you to have second thoughts. Firstly, it had been generally assumed that the sword in the stone was a comparatively modern, if clever, fabrication. However, based on the composition of the metal, and the style of the sword, research has determined that the sword does in fact date from the twelfth century CE. Secondly, the chapel also contains a more gruesome relic: a pair of mummified hands. According to legend, the devil wanted San Galgano dead, and so sent someone to assassinate him. Apparently, this would-be hitman was attacked by a pack of wolves while en route and was killed. It is supposedly the hands of this unfortunate individual that reside in the chapel. Alternatively, another legend concerning the macabre hands maintains that anyone who tries to remove the sword will have their hands ripped off. In this version, we are therefore presumably presented with the remnants of an unsuccessful attempt at sword retrieval. In either case, the mummified remains have been radiocarbon-dated to – yes, you've guessed it – the twelfth century CE!

Ground-penetrating radar has also revealed a 2 by 1 metre cavity beneath the sword-bearing stone. Could this be the resting place of San Galgano himself? It would seem logical but, to date, no excavation has taken place.

Clearly, while any sensible person will take this story with a very large pinch of salt, it does seem as though curious things were happening at Montesiepi around 800 years ago. But how do we get from a Mediterranean nobleman, born in 1148, to a legendary King of England, reputed to have lived over half a millennium earlier?

To put it simply, what is the correlation between twelfth-century Italy and fifth-century England? Well, it is probably no coincidence that Geoffrey of Monmouth was writing his *Historia Regum Britanniae* around the time that the events described above were supposedly occurring. Might Geoffrey have learned of the San Galgano story and simply decided to embellish the Arthurian legend with an anglicised version of the old sword in the stone routine?

It is possible that a king who went by the name of Arthur did indeed walk upon England's pastures green. But I am fairly certain that, if he existed at all, he never extracted a sword from a solid piece of rock. And yet, in Montesiepi there is a solid piece of rock with a sword firmly encased in it. It's a funny old world!

SEVEN

THE HOUSE THAT SARAH BUILT

Sarah Pardee was beautiful and charming, musically talented, and fluent in several languages. She lived with her parents in New Haven, Connecticut, in the USA. Born in 1839, she was, by the 1860s, well known in social circles, and her company was sought after by many of the town's eligible bachelors. The young man who won her heart was one William Wirt Winchester, the son of prominent local businessman Oliver Winchester.

The happy couple were married on 30 September 1862, and their future could not have seemed rosier. Oliver Winchester had developed the first true repeating rifle and, with the outbreak of the American Civil War on 12 April 1861, it was an extremely profitable time to be a manufacturer of state-of-the-art weaponry. Winchester Senior soon amassed a large fortune, to which William was the heir.

On 15 July 1866, Sarah gave birth to a daughter and named her Annie. Tragically, the baby almost immediately contracted a wasting disease, and by 24 July she was dead. Sarah was devastated at her loss, and her behaviour was such that concerns were expressed about her mental health. In fact, it was almost a decade before she made a substantial recovery, and the couple never had another child.

Sarah Winchester in 1865

Oliver Winchester passed away on 11 December 1880, and William inherited his father's fortune. However, tragedy was to strike one more time, as William developed tuberculosis and died on 7 March 1881. And so it was that the grief-stricken widow came to be worth more than 20 million dollars, or about 450 million dollars in today's terms. A staggering sum of money. Additionally, Sarah received 48.9% of the Winchester Repeating Arms Company and an income of about 1,000 dollars per day – approximately 22,000 dollars in current terms.

However, Sarah remained a troubled woman, grieving for the loss of her husband and not completely recovered from the death of her daughter 15 years earlier. A friend suggested that she should seek solace by consulting a medium. Not an advisable course of action but, in her fragile state of mind, she was desperate to alleviate her grief, and the thought of being able to communicate with her departed loved ones must have appealed to her. Spiritualism was at the height of its popularity during the late nineteenth century.

The encounter with the medium was a disaster. The name of the individual is not recorded, but he or she either had a grudge against Sarah or her family, or had no clue as to the consequences of the information they were about to impart. "Your husband is here," the medium began, and continued: "He says for me to tell you that there is a curse on your family, which took the life of he and your child. It will soon take you too. It is a curse that has resulted from the terrible weapon created by the Winchester family. Thousands of people have died because of it, and their spirits are now seeking vengeance."

As the seance continued, Sarah was told to sell her house in New Haven and head west, where she would be guided by her husband until she found her new home. The encounter concluded with the medium telling her: "You must start a new life and build a home for yourself and for the spirits who have fallen from this terrible weapon too. You can never stop building the house. If you continue building, you will live. Stop and you will die."

Many people would simply have dismissed the curse as nonsense. The trouble was that Sarah believed every word! She sold her house, as instructed, and set off westwards, eventually reaching the Santa Clara Valley in California in 1884. Here she came upon a house under construction and entered into negotiations to purchase the partly built home and all 162 acres of land associated with it. The owner, a Dr Caldwell, quickly agreed to sell; she presumably having made him an offer he couldn't refuse. Sarah immediately dispensed with the original plans for the house and embarked on her own unprecedented construction project that would continue 24 hours a day for nigh on 38 years!

Sarah never employed an architect, nor did she draw up a master plan for the house. Instead, she met daily with the foreman and presented him with a hand-sketched plan for the day's work. Her design, such as it was, was for a house that would confuse the spirits that she was obliged to share it with and so discourage them from doing her harm. Numerous staircases and corridors were constructed that led nowhere; there were cupboards that opened to reveal only the wall; upstairs doors that opened to sheer drops to the ground level below; and fireplaces with chimneys that did not even reach the ceiling! The house would eventually contain many other bizarre design features, such as a staircase with 42 steps that rose less than one storey high because each step was just 2 inches high!

By 1906, Sarah's idiosyncratic project had reached an astonishing seven storeys in height. But disaster was just around the corner. In that same year, the San Francisco earthquake caused the top three floors to collapse. Fortunately, the rest of the house suffered less severe damage and work quickly commenced to repair what remained. The top three floors, however, were never rebuilt. Sarah took the earthquake to be a sign that the spirits were furious that the house was nearing completion, and so the construction continued apace.

On the morning of 5 September 1922, Sarah was found dead in her bed. She had died in her sleep the

Winchester House

previous night, at the age of 83. At last, the hammers and saws fell silent. Today, the house is a popular tourist attraction. However, a couple of mysteries remain unanswered. So confusing is the interior, no one seems able to agree on how many rooms it contains. Certainly, there are at least 148, although many claim to have counted up to 160. You may like to try and count them yourself, if you ever get the chance to pay the Winchester House a visit. And what of the spirits that so troubled Sarah? Surely just the product of a disturbed mind. But what if the medium was right? It might not be just the rooms you find yourself counting!

EIGHT

DAN DONNELLY'S ARM

On a cold wet night in February 1820, an intoxicated man staggered out of a Dublin bar and collapsed nearby. By the time the drenched and shivering man was discovered the following morning, he was in a bad way; within a few days he was dead. And so it was that pneumonia claimed the life of Dan Donnelly, Ireland's unbeaten heavyweight bare-knuckle boxing champion. He was just 31 years of age.

Supposedly born on 17 March 1788 – St Patrick's Day – Dan had 16 siblings and was the son of a carpenter. Although brought up in relative poverty, he grew tall and strong, and at around 6 feet in height and approximately 200 pounds in weight he was a big man by the standards of the day. The majority of the population at that time were undernourished and as a consequence tended to be much smaller and lighter than today. People of under 5 feet in height were not uncommon.

Dan Donnelly

As a young man, Dan gained a reputation as a formidable fist fighter. Stories were told of his heroics as a dispatcher of bullies, and protector of those less capable than himself. How much of this was true is a matter for conjecture. Such tales would undoubtedly have served to embellish his growing reputation as a local hero, but there is no doubt that he was more than capable of taking care of himself.

Donnelly's first foray into the world of prize fighting came on 14 September 1814. The venue was a natural amphitheatre known as 'Belcher's Hollow', in County Kildare. His opponent was Tom Hall, an English boxer who was undertaking a tour of Ireland. Such was Dan's burgeoning reputation that an enormous crowd, estimated at 20,000, gathered to watch the spectacle. To the delight of the partisan attendees, in round 15 Donnelly was awarded the fight by the referee, with Hall refusing to continue.

His next fight was against another Englishman: the hugely experienced George Cooper. This took place on 13 December 1815. The venue was the same as his first fight, but it had now been renamed Donnelly's Hollow, in Dan's honour. Cooper was outweighed by approximately 20 pounds but used his experience to outfox his heavier opponent. However, Donnelly's superior strength eventually told, and Cooper was knocked unconscious by a huge right-hand punch in round 11.

His third, and what transpired to be his last, fight took place near London at a place called Crawley

Hurst. Dan had been on a tour of England but, being short of money, had agreed to meet Tom Oliver, another experienced English fighter. The match took place on 21 July 1819. This turned out to be a gruelling encounter, with Donnelly eventually emerging victorious after 34 rounds.

Within a year, Dan was dead. His career as a prize fighter was not prolific, but he was unbeaten. There are not many boxers who can claim a 100% record! But it is not only for his pugilistic prowess that he is mainly remembered today. Donnelly was unfortunate enough to die at a time when the medical profession was just starting to realise that many illnesses were due to pathological changes occurring inside the body. To further their understanding, surgeons were keen to obtain cadavers on which they could carry out autopsies and dissections. Keen to meet this demand, unscrupulous individuals took to robbing the graves of the recently interred and selling them on to surgeons, who must have been only too well aware of the practice. This was the fate of poor Dan's body.

As a much-lamented son of Ireland, it was not long before visitors to his graveside noticed that his resting place had been disturbed. Uproar ensued and, shortly thereafter, a surgeon by the name of Doctor Hall confessed to having possession of the body. Apparently, he had not initially recognised the corpse as being that of the famed fighter, and he immediately gave an assurance that he would re-inter Dan's mortal remains. This he did, with the exception of the late fighter's right arm! Apparently, the surgeon wanted to conduct medical tests on the arm that had dispatched the English fighters. Accounts differ as to whether this omission was made with or without the permission of Donnelly's admirers.

To preserve the arm, it was coated in red lead paint, and it subsequently found its way to Scotland, where it was used as a teaching aid at Edinburgh University for around 50 years. The mummified arm was then sold to a travelling circus which displayed the gruesome artefact on tours of England, until it was again sold, this time to a Belfast publican in 1904. Over the course of the twentieth century, it spent most of the time on display in a couple of public houses in Ireland. When the last of these establishments changed hands (no pun intended), the arm was removed from display, and it turned up next in New York as part of an exhibition of fighting Irishmen. The arm returned home to Ireland in 2009 and, to date, continues to make appearances at exhibitions of boxing memorabilia. Compared to Dan himself, who left the Emerald Isle only once in his lifetime, his right arm has put in some serious mileage over the years!

NINE

THE UNKNOWN CHILD

The CS *Mackay-Bennett* was a cable repair ship that operated primarily in the North Atlantic between 1884 and 1922. Now, mending underwater cables is not a terribly interesting subject to be writing about, I agree, but it is the *Mackay-Bennett*'s role in the aftermath of one of the twentieth century's most infamous tragedies for which she is remembered today.

The ship was commissioned from John Elder & Co, a shipbuilder based on the River Clyde in Glasgow, Scotland. Launched in September 1884, she incorporated a number of innovative features. Being a cable ship, an abnormally deep keel was required to be able to store as much cable as possible. Bilge keels, which aid stability in rough seas, were added to either side of the hull to help cope with the notoriously treacherous Atlantic Ocean, and she was also fitted with two rudders – one at the front, in addition to the traditional one at the rear – to increase manoeuvrability.

The CS Mackay-Bennett

The CS *Mackay-Bennett* was also one of the first ships to be built from steel.

The ship operated mainly out of Halifax, Nova Scotia, but occasionally also from Plymouth, England, when working on cables on the European side of the Atlantic. Being designed to cope with rough seas, and often working far out into the ocean, she was also able to assist in several rescues of stricken vessels, saving many lives in the process. However, it is not for one of these rescues that the CS *Mackay-Bennett* sealed her place in history.

In April 1912, she was carrying out maintenance on the France to Canada communications cable when she was requisitioned by the White Star Line to undertake a far more sombre task. On the night of 14 April 1912, the RMS *Titanic* struck an iceberg on her maiden voyage and rapidly sank. Of the approximately 2,200 passengers and crew, only 706 would survive the disaster. This meant that there lay a grim task ahead: the recovery of as many bodies of dead passengers and crew as possible.

RMS Titanic

The CS *Mackay-Bennett* returned to Halifax, emptied her cable stores and, in place of the usual load, took on board 100 coffins, 100 tons of ice for storing the recovered bodies, and embalming supplies for 70 corpses. In addition, they also took with them Canon Kenneth Cameron Hind of All Saints Cathedral, Halifax, and John R Snow Jr, chief embalmer of Nova Scotia's largest undertaking firm.

Departing Halifax on Wednesday, 17 April 1912, the ship encountered rough seas and thick fog and, as a consequence, took nearly four days to reach the site of the sinking – a distance of around 800 nautical miles. Recovery of the bodies began at 6am on 20 April, when lifeboats were offloaded and rowed into the area where the *Titanic* went down. The lifeboat crews were both surprised and disturbed by the number of bodies, and hauled as many as they deemed safe into the boats. They returned to the ship with 51 corpses. Over the course of seven days, the lifeboats would recover a total of 306 bodies. Only 328 bodies were ever recovered from the scene of the disaster, making the CS *Mackay-Bennett* responsible for more than 90% of those reclaimed from the water. However, there was a problem.

It soon became apparent to the captain that there was insufficient space aboard to store all of the recovered bodies. He therefore introduced a system that would be regarded as elitist and wholly unacceptable by today's standards. Namely, that first-class passengers would be embalmed and placed in coffins, second-class passengers would be embalmed and wrapped in canvas, and third-class passengers would be buried at sea. This approach was deemed appropriate at the time and, while clearly biased in favour of the better-off, nevertheless solved the storage problem.

Among the first-class passengers recovered were Isidor Straus, owner of Macy's department store, and John Jacob Astor IV, the richest man on board the *Titanic*. They also recovered the body of Wallace Hartley, the bandleader who continued to play on as the ship sank. Most poignantly, however, the remains of just one third-class passenger were saved by the crew and stored in the hold. It was the body of a small boy, aged approximately two years. Of the 306 bodies recovered, 116 were buried at sea and 190 brought back to Halifax, where they arrived on 30 April 1912. It is largely thanks to Clifford Crease, a crewman of the CS *Mackay-Bennett*, that we have such detailed information of the recovery operation. His personal diary, detailing the events, is now held in the Public Archives of Nova Scotia.

Sadly, the body of the child remained unclaimed, and so the unknown boy was laid to rest in Halifax, with the crew of the CS *Mackay-Bennett* paying for the burial and headstone from their own wages. In addition, the coffin was marked by a copper plaque inscribed 'Our Babe'. The entire crew, and most of the population of Halifax, attended the child's funeral on 4 May 1912.

Almost a century later, the copper plaque was to play a pivotal role in the identification of the unknown child. When the body was exhumed for testing, it was the remains that had been preserved beneath the plaque that yielded sufficient DNA for identification purposes. On 30 July 2007, the child was revealed as Sidney Leslie Goodwin, a 19-month-old from Wiltshire in England. His entire family had perished in the sinking.

The CS *Mackay-Bennett* was retired in May 1922 and anchored in

John Jacob Astor IV

Plymouth Sound, where she was used for storage. She was finally scrapped in 1963.

Clifford Crease never forgot the child he had helped to bury. During his lifetime, he visited the grave on every anniversary of the tragedy. When he passed away in 1961, he was interred only a few metres from the boy whose name he never knew.

TEN

THE MEMORY OF WATER

Have you ever wondered, as you sip your mineral water in a pub garden on a warm summer's evening, who first thought that it would be a good idea to start drinking the stuff that flows down mountain streams? Well, possibly not. If you are anything like me, you are more likely to be wondering why you have just paid the best part of £2 for a glass of water!

With this in mind, I resolved to go in search of the culprit responsible for relieving me of my hard-earned readies. As seems to be the case with most of these things, it soon became apparent that our penchant for mountain spring water is the result of an accumulation of factors, rather than any single identifiable eureka moment. Certainly, to point the finger of blame in any one direction would be a little unfair, but the earliest perpetrator in this case of global mugging appears to have been a grumpy, iconoclastic medical reformer, who went by the name of Paracelsus.

Paracelsus was born Phillip von Hohenheim in Switzerland in 1493, but modestly rebranded himself 'Paracelsus', meaning 'greater than Celsus' (a first-century Roman encyclopaedist). Paracelsus appears to have been the first person to reject the medical theories of the ancients: the notion that health was maintained by a careful balancing of the four bodily 'humours'. According to the ancient Greek Hippocrates and his Roman counterpart Galen, if you were ill it was because you were too hot, cold, wet or dry! It was the job of the learned physician to rebalance the humours and so restore health.

Instead, Paracelsus resolutely believed that diseases were caused by external factors, such as poisons emitted by stars, or minerals in the earth. To treat such maladies, he prescribed chemical remedies derived from the very rocks and minerals that he thought responsible for the ailment. His ideas were firmly rejected by the traditionally educated medical elite of the day, who relied instead on the panacea of bloodletting, or on herbal remedies that caused patients to purge or vomit, as preferred treatments for the humourally imbalanced.

As an itinerant medical practitioner, Paracelsus travelled extensively, and seems to have found himself in trouble with authority wherever he went. He was widely regarded by the medical profession as an alchemist and a mountebank: one who peddled untested remedies from the roadside. While this may give the impression of a lonely wanderer at odds with the world, as his nomenclature suggests, he was no wallflower, and certainly did not lack confidence. From his selected writings we are informed thus: *"Let me tell you this*: every little hair on my neck knows more

than you and all your scribes." He was also boastful
with regard to his 'experienced' beard, although,
paradoxically, he appears clean-shaven in portraits. A
hypothetical beard, perhaps!

Paracelsian medicine flourished after his death in
1541, but ultimately failed to unseat humoural theory
as the basis of accepted medical practice. However,
his legacy was that his mineral-based remedies were
eventually incorporated into the pharmacopoeia of
traditional medicine. He also helped pave the way for
subsequent generations of chemists, who were able
to flourish because time had shown that his chemical
treatments were actually beneficial and not just the
useless products of a cantankerous fool.

"All very interesting," you might, or might not,
say, 'but what has all this got to do with my glass of
spring water?" Well, it was Paracelsus' use of chemical
remedies that led to a more scientific approach to
medicine in general (known as 'the iatrochemical
revolution', in case you were wondering). During the
course of the sixteenth century, physicians and natural
philosophers (the term 'scientist' was still a long way
off) began collating information on the properties
of water from locations across Europe. The Italian
physician, Andrea Bacci, and the Swiss botanist,
Conrad Gesner, both undertook wide-ranging studies
of the natural environment and quickly realised that
water from different locations contained different
properties. Water could thus be used in the treatment
of various ailments, depending on the constitution of
metals or minerals contained therein.

Towards the end of the sixteenth century,
physicians began prescribing mineral water, to be

either drunk or bathed in, as a means of rebalancing the humours. It was not long before the commercial potential of the seemingly limitless supply was realised. During the seventeenth and eighteenth centuries, spa towns sprung up all over Europe, and their water was bottled and sold for considerable profit. Those wealthy enough could travel to such fashionable resorts as Spa in modern-day Belgium, Vichy in France, or Bath in England, and could drink and bathe with impunity.

Those unable to travel to such places, due to poverty or frailty, could still partake of the waters thanks to the selfless entrepreneurs prepared to bottle, transport and sell the water for as much as they felt able to charge. Not only were such sources exploited for profit but, more shocking even than that, counterfeiters moved in on the trade. It seems as though Peckham spring water was but a relatively recent addition to a long-established tradition!

Today, the subject of commercial rights to naturally occurring mineral water remains a controversial topic, and many mineral waters are now even prepared synthetically, with the mineral content being added to ordinary water! But, by and large, it seems as though it is really only a minority of miserable whingers like myself who still complain about paying excessive amounts of money for H2O + a bit of rock. It seems we buy the bottled stuff in unbelievable volumes: more than 288 billion litres* was sold

Paracelsus (1493–1541)

globally in 2012. So, as you sip your glass of mineral water, spare a thought for the man who inadvertently pioneered a multi-billion-pound industry, and raise your glass in a toast. To Paracelsus!

ELEVEN

SCRATCHING FANNY: THE COCK LANE GHOST

"Titter ye not," as the late British comedian Frankie Howerd would have said. This particular tale takes us back to a time when Fanny was nothing more than an abbreviated form of the name 'Frances' and, as you will be aware, a cock is a male chicken. Okay, now that we've cleared that up, on with the story.

In the year 1756, a young man by the name of William Kent got married in Norfolk, in the east of England. William and his bride, one Elizabeth Lynes, almost immediately moved to London. Sadly, Elizabeth died in childbirth in 1757, and their baby passed away only a short time later. Stricken with grief, William turned to Elizabeth's sister, Frances, also known as 'Fanny', for solace. She had been living with them in the capacity of housekeeper.

One thing led to another, and the two were soon romantically involved. As Fanny was William's sister-in-law, they were not, at that time, permitted to marry. Consequently, the couple decided to 'live in sin'. While this was not a socially acceptable arrangement in the middle of the eighteenth century, the couple decided that, since they hailed from distant Norfolk, it was unlikely their secret would come to light in such a busy and bustling metropolis. Subsequently, they moved from the rented accommodation they had shared with Elizabeth and set up home as man and wife.

Their new home was at 33 Cock Lane, where they rented some rooms from the owner of the property: a Richard Parsons. Parsons had a reputation as a drunk, and was habitually short of money, owing to his excessive drinking. Parsons soon approached William for a loan, and borrowed the sum of 12 guineas, promising to repay the money in monthly instalments. A guinea was a sum of money equivalent to one pound and one shilling, and 12 guineas would equate to about £2,500 in today's terms. For some reason, William must have trusted the oft-sozzled Parsons because not only did he lend him quite a large sum of money, but he also confided in him that he and Fanny were not actually married. William Kent would live to regret his naivety.

A nineteenth-century illustration of Cock Lane

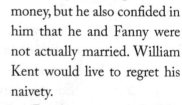

By the autumn of 1759, Fanny was pregnant and, when William announced that he needed to go away on business for a few days, she expressed concern at being left alone in her delicate condition. As a result, William made arrangements for Parsons' 11-year-old daughter Elizabeth to stay with Fanny for the duration of his absence.

It was at this point that events took a purportedly paranormal turn. Their sleep was disturbed by knocking or scratching sounds that began emanating from the wall to an adjoining property. As a cobbler lived next door, Fanny assumed he was simply working late in order to clear a backlog of work. However, when the sounds continued on the following Sunday night, when Fanny knew the house next door was empty, she began to assign a supernatural explanation to the noises. Whether William agreed with Fanny's interpretation of the events is unclear. However, he did make arrangements for him and Fanny to move to new accommodation.

As Parsons had not even begun to repay the loan, William instructed a solicitor to take legal action against him to recover his money. Parsons, by way of retaliation, elected to betray William's confidence, and made it known to all and sundry that William Kent and Fanny Lynes were not legally married. He even claimed that the knocking and scratching sounds were caused by William's deceased wife, Elizabeth, seeking revenge for the unprincipled behaviour of her widowed husband.

Unfortunately, fate had not yet finished with William and was to deal him one more blow. Tragically, Fanny contracted smallpox, and by February 1760 she was dead, along with her unborn child. Parsons, who claimed that the unearthly noises had continued at his property, despite the fact that William was no longer living there, now claimed that the sounds were messages from Elizabeth *and* possibly also her sister, the recently deceased Fanny. An unusual example of poltergeist nepotism, presumably!

It was around this time that Parsons began conducting seances, encouraged by a Methodist minister, the Reverend John Moore, who was keen to prove the existence of an afterlife through contact with the deceased. During these seances, Parsons claimed to have contacted the spirit of Fanny, who, through knocking, asserted that she had in fact been murdered by William Kent and that the method he had employed was arsenic poisoning. William soon heard about the seances and decided it would be in his best interests to attend any future gatherings in person.

At one such meeting, Parsons declared that Fanny had proclaimed that William Kent would be hanged for her murder. William was by now ready to deal with Parsons' absurd allegations and had brought with him his solicitor as well as the pharmacist who had cared for Fanny during her illness. However, despite their confirmations that Fanny had indeed died of smallpox, many in the community believed Parsons and demanded that William pay for his crime with his life. It was at this point that the press gave the ghost of Cock Lane the nickname 'Scratching Fanny'.

Such was the furore that the Lord Mayor of London became involved, and he decided to sort things out once and for all. He noticed that Parsons' daughter, Elizabeth, always seemed to be present

A nineteenth-century illustration of the haunted room

when the knocking and scratching occurred. After protracted questioning, Elizabeth confessed to producing the noises herself, by means of a wooden board that she kept hidden under her bed. Initially, she had only intended to frighten Fanny; but once her father had realised that he could use Elizabeth's trickery to avoid repaying his debt to William Kent, he colluded with his daughter to implicate Kent in Fanny's demise.

As if further proof were needed, the investigating committee decided to visit the crypt in which Fanny had been interred. The notion being that if Fanny was capable of producing disembodied knocking sounds in the walls of 33 Cock Lane it would surely be a piece of cake for her to knock on her own coffin lid! Needless to say, with Elizabeth Parsons not in attendance Fanny failed to respond when requested to make her presence known.

William Kent's reputation was thus restored, and he went on to live an otherwise unremarkable life with his new wife Bathsheba. Parsons and the Reverend Moore were arrested, and Parsons was imprisoned for two years. Additionally, he and the inept reverend were made to pay damages of almost £600 to William – more than £100,000 in current terms. How Richard Parsons must have lived to regret welching on the loan!

A couple of additional facts about Cock Lane that might be of interest to you: firstly, it was the point at which the Great Fire of

Cock Lane in the twenty-first century

London finally burned itself out in 1666; and secondly, during the medieval period Cock Lane was the site of a large number of brothels. Upon reflection, my assertion about a poultry-related source for the name may have been somewhat wide of the mark! Oh, all right, go on then. Ye may titter, after all!

TWELVE

THE SURPRISING HISTORY OF EVERYDAY WORDS

Language evolves over time. If we were able to converse with our ancestors from five or six generations removed, we would be quite surprised at how many words we use today that they would not recognise. Conversely, words also fall out of use, and we would be equally bemused by some of the archaic vocabulary of our forefathers. With this in mind, I decided to look into the etymologies of a few everyday words, the origins of which I had hitherto never given a second thought. What follows are some examples of word origins that I found particularly interesting. I hope you agree.

There's a fair chance that you may have a 'death contract'. Yes, if you have an outstanding loan on a property you have bought, I'm talking about you! The word 'mortgage' is derived from French law and literally means 'death contract or pledge'. Fortunately, the death bit refers to the demise of the contract, upon

Ouch!

either the final repayment, or seizure of the property through foreclosure, rather than to the expiration of the borrower. I am, however, reminded of one or two tightwads I have known down the years who would probably have regarded snuffing it mid mortgage as something of a result!

Today, when we hear the word 'avocado', we tend to think of a posh fruit. But it wasn't always thus; oh no! Avocado derives from an Aztec word '*ahuacatl*', the meaning of which is 'testicle'. Presumably the Aztecs so named the fruit because of its resemblance in shape rather than size. Anyone with avocado-sized testicles would be in serious trouble!

A 'saboteur' is someone who commits an act of sabotage, right? Well yes, except that the word originally meant something completely different. Today, 'sabotage' means to deliberately obstruct or destroy, but the word started out, believe it or not, in footwear. Beginning life in thirteenth-century France, 'sabots' were wooden shoes, or clogs, I suppose we would call them today.

A sabot maker

Compared to the more fashionable and expensive leather shoes, sabots were considered by the better-off as the preserve of the oafish, peasant classes. People walking in wooden shoes tend to make a lot of noise, and the term 'saboter' came to mean someone who walked noisily in sabots.

Quite how we get from saboter to saboteur, meaning 'obstructer' or 'destroyer', is not certain, but there is a good story that could explain it. The mechanisation of manual tasks, that resulted from the Industrial Revolution, was not universally welcomed. While the rate of production increased significantly, and profits soared, the new industrial processes were less labour intensive and so fewer people were required in the workplace. Understandably, workers were more than a little displeased at finding themselves surplus to requirements and some decided to take matters into their own hands. Apparently, they threw their sabots into the mechanisms of the new-fangled machines in order to 'clog' them up and stop them from working. Hence the machinery was sabotaged! Unfortunately, there is no primary source of historical evidence to verify this tale, but never let the truth get in the way of a good story, I always say!

Approximately one-third of babies are delivered by 'caesarean' section, but where does the name come from? Legend has it that the Roman general and politician, Julius Caesar, was born this way and that he is therefore the origin of the word 'caesarean'. However, it is almost certain that his mother gave birth to him naturally. Under Roman law, the delivery of babies by way of cutting open the mother was reserved either for women who had died in childbirth or in order to save a child's life, where severe complications had arisen during the delivery. There is, however, no evidence to suggest that any mother actually survived the procedure, and the mother of Julius Caesar, Aurelia Cotta, was still alive when her son reached adulthood. Indeed, the first known case of a woman surviving such a procedure was not recorded until the sixteenth

Julius Caesar

century, when a Swiss pig castrator used his skills on his wife to deliver their child in this way.

So, if the word is not derived from Julius Caesar, then where did it come from? Well, it turns out that we were in the right neck of the woods all along. In Latin, the word *'caedo'* means 'to cut', and so it would appear that it does indeed come down to us from Roman times; it just derives from a humble verb. There is, however, one further complication that could explain how the confusion with Julius Caesar arose. The Roman author, Pliny the Elder, makes reference to someone named 'Caesar' being born by caesarean section, but he is actually referring to a remote ancestor of the Roman general. Pliny goes on to say that he "was so named from his having been removed by an incision in his mother's womb." So, it would appear that the whole thing may have been turned on its head. It is the name 'Caesar' that derives from a caesarean birth, not the other way around!

Just before we leave the Roman era, the word 'addict' meant 'slave' in Latin. Today, we use the word to refer to a person who has become a slave *to* something, rather than *of* someone.

The word 'denim' has its origin in the French city of Nimes. The cloth was originally called *'serge de Nimes'*, meaning 'fabric from Nimes'. The word *'serge'* was quickly dropped, leaving just *'de Nimes'*. The word 'jeans' is similarly derived from its place of origin: the Italian city of Genoa.

'Jumbo' is thought to have been a West African word meaning 'elephant'. In English, it came to mean something very big only after an African elephant named Jumbo arrived at London Zoo in 1860. Sadly, Jumbo died as the result of a railway accident in 1885. He was being exercised when he stumbled and fell on to train tracks and was struck by a passing locomotive.

THIRTEEN

THE RISE AND FALL OF JEAN-PIERRE BLANCHARD

As pioneers of aviation go, Jean-Pierre Blanchard may not be the first name that springs to mind, but it was certainly not for the want of trying. Born in Les Andelys, France, in 1753, Blanchard was both an inventor and a shameless self-publicist. Early in his career he designed and constructed a variation on the velocipede: a forerunner of the bicycle, but without pedals. As a further development to his design, he added not only the much-needed pedals but also flapping wings and oars. Yes, the intrepid Monsieur Blanchard had invented a flying bicycle!

Needless to say, it didn't work. Undeterred, however, he claimed to have made several successful flights aboard his invention, although none of course were witnessed, and no one believed him. However, his attention was soon drawn to a method of flying that really did work. Following the success of the

Montgolfier brothers' experiments with hot air balloons – Etienne Montgolfier being the first person to be lifted clear of the earth in 1783 – Blanchard was hot on their heels, so to speak. By March 1784, he had built a hydrogen balloon and, eager to improve on the Montgolfiers' efforts, fitted it out with his trademark flapping wings, air screws and oars. Persistent and single-minded was the audacious Blanchard.

An example of a velocipede

Eager for publicity, and keen to improve his financial situation, Blanchard decided to move his operations to England: virgin territory for ballooning, and well away from the overbearing shadow of the Montgolfiers. In London, he began taking fare-paying passengers for rides in his balloon. Not everyone was pleased with his efforts, though. A Dr Sheldon hired him and his aerial contraption to take weather-measuring instruments, including a barometer, up into the atmosphere to conduct some serious scientific experiments. To the doctor's consternation, however, Blanchard, realising that he was losing height, elected to jettison the expensive but heavy equipment in order to gain altitude. The conversation between doctor and balloonist upon Blanchard's return to earth was sadly not recorded!

On the other hand, Dr John Jeffries, a wealthy physician, was far more impressed with Blanchard's ballooning skills than his meteorological counterpart. After enjoying a balloon flight with our hero, Jeffries got talking to Blanchard and they decided upon an attempt to be the first people in history to fly across the

Jean-Pierre Blanchard

English Channel. With Jeffries' money behind the scheme, and Blanchard's ballooning brilliance, what could possibly go wrong? Well, Blanchard, for one thing!

After a three-week wait for favourable winds, perfect weather conditions finally arrived on 7 January 1785. The party duly assembled at Dover Castle in England, and excitement grew, along with the balloon, as it began to inflate. Blanchard, however, had his own agenda. He didn't want to be just *one* of the first people to cross the Channel by air; he wanted to be *the* first person to cross the Channel by means other than water. His first ruse was to barricade himself in a room at Dover Castle and refuse to come out. His strategy, such as it was, seems to have been based on the assumption that Jeffries would soon tire of waiting and simply leave. He didn't!

Blanchard was eventually coaxed out of his self-imposed confinement following the intervention of the castle's governor. Undeterred, he moved on to Plan B. With the balloon refusing to lift off, Blanchard claimed that it was because the combined weight of the two men was too much and that, in the circumstances, he had no choice but to undertake the dangerous task alone. Jeffries, by now suspicious of Blanchard's motives, frisked the balloonist and discovered him to have a pouch-belt filled with lead shot concealed about his waist. Alleviated of this additional weight, the balloon, with both men aboard, began to rise.

Heading out over the Channel, however, things did not go quite as planned. It transpired that the balloon really was carrying too much weight, and the pair found themselves practically skimming the waves. Despite jettisoning all of the ballast weights, the balloon was still not gaining altitude, and so they also ditched the wooden decorations that adorned the gondola. Still dangerously low, Blanchard finally conceded, and threw out his beloved, but useless, oars and air screws.

Approaching the French coast, it became apparent to Blanchard that they were still not high enough and were in real danger of crashing. In what must have been a very careful manoeuvre, both men evacuated their bowels and bladders into the sea before also throwing their clothes overboard. Mercifully, that did the trick, and the balloon was just able to clear a clump of trees that had been threatening disaster and land safely on French soil. Dressed only in their underwear, the unlikely looking and chilly heroes had taken around two and a half hours to complete the crossing, and in so doing wrote their names into the record books.

Despite achieving international fame, the cross-Channel adventure seems to have marked the end of Dr Jeffries' career as a balloonist because shortly thereafter he resumed his medical practice, which he continued until his death in 1819. Blanchard, on the other hand, was quick to exploit his new-found notoriety and embarked on a European tour with his balloon. He subsequently became the first person to fly in a balloon in Belgium, the Netherlands, Germany and Poland; and, on 9 January 1793, he took off from Philadelphia, Pennsylvania, in the first ever balloon flight in the Americas.

Blanchard and Jeffries head out over the water

Later in his career, Blanchard began experimenting with parachutes, initially by dropping cats and dogs from his balloon. Even assuming they floated harmlessly to earth, the poor creatures would presumably have found the experience terrifying! He was later able to try one out for himself when his balloon canopy ruptured during a flight.

As you might imagine, his eventual demise was also balloon related. On 20 February 1808, at The Hague in the Netherlands, Blanchard was in the process of launching his balloon when he suffered a heart attack and fell from the gondola from a height of approximately 50 feet. He subsequently succumbed to his injuries at the age of 55. A braggart and shameless self-publicist, without doubt; the world nevertheless needs people like Jean-Pierre Blanchard. I hope you agree!

FOURTEEN

THE REMARKABLE WAR OF LANCE CORPORAL WILLIAM HAROLD COLTMAN

Prior to the outbreak of World War I, the life of Bill Coltman had been unexceptional. Born in Staffordshire, England, on 17 November 1891, he was a market gardener by trade and taught at his local village Sunday school. As a member of the Plymouth Brethren, his religious persuasion meant that he held a predominantly pacifistic outlook on life. All in all, there was nothing about Bill to suggest that his participation in the approaching conflict would be significant.

Indeed, it was due to his strong religious beliefs that, upon enlisting for service in 1915, he registered as a conscientious objector and requested to serve only in a non-combatant role. His request was duly granted, and he was assigned to the post of stretcher-bearer with the North Staffordshire (Prince of Wales) Regiment. As he would soon discover, the role actually

Bill Coltman

placed him in much greater danger than his combatant colleagues. He was frequently obliged to carry out rescue missions across the hellish and brutal terrain of no-man's-land, without any means with which to defend himself, while others remained ensconced in the comparative safety of the trenches.

He soon began to build a reputation for bravery and dedication to duty, refusing rest until all those wounded in action had been recovered. Despite being only 5 feet 4 inches in height and of slim build, he often operated on his own, carrying injured soldiers from the battlefield on his back. He was frequently mentioned in dispatches, and his exemplary service was recognised by the French Army, which decorated him with the Croix de Guerre: a medal awarded to individuals who distinguish themselves through acts of heroism.

Following the rescue of a wounded officer from no-man's-land, Bill Coltman was awarded the Military Medal in February 1917. In June of 1917, when mortar fire set light to a store, he removed the stock of hand grenades held therein, thus preventing a much deadlier conflagration. He also rescued a number of men trapped in a collapsed tunnel; and in recognition of his actions, a bar was added to his Military Medal. In July 1917, Bill was in action once again, this time risking his life to evacuate injured soldiers from the front line while under heavy shelling. He even continued to search for wounded colleagues throughout the hours of darkness, despite continuing shell and machine-gun fire. In recognition of his bravery, he was awarded the Distinguished Conduct Medal. The year 1917, it seems, was a momentous year in the life of the young man from Staffordshire.

If 1917 had been a remarkable year for Bill, 1918, as it turned out, would be no less memorable. In September of that year, while under heavy artillery fire, he administered treatment to the injured and carried many wounded men to safety over a period of some 24 hours, refusing to rest until he was certain there were no more casualties requiring help. For this selfless bravery, he was awarded a bar to his Distinguished Conduct Medal. And, as if all of that was not enough, his finest hour was yet to come.

Towards the end of the war, a number of wounded soldiers had to be left on open ground following a retreat. Learning of this, Bill ventured forward alone in the face of heavy crossfire and, on three separate occasions, carried injured servicemen on his back until safely behind Allied defences, undoubtedly saving their lives. During this engagement, he also worked continuously for 48 hours, treating the wounded. In recognition of his incredible courage, Bill Coltman earned the highest award for gallantry that can be awarded to a British serviceman: the Victoria Cross.

And so it was that Lance Corporal William Harold Coltman VC, DCM and Bar, MM and Bar became Britain's most decorated enlisted soldier of World War I, despite the fact that, throughout the entire conflict, he was not wounded and never fired a single shot in anger!

As is typical of men of his calibre, Bill shied away from the limelight. On 22 May 1919, he was invested with his Victoria Cross by King George

V at Buckingham Palace, following which he went straight home in order to avoid a civic reception held in his honour in his hometown of Burton-on-Trent, Staffordshire. After the war, he took up employment with his local authority parks department as a groundskeeper, a position he held until his retirement in 1963.

Bill Coltman died on 29 June 1974, aged 82. His grave, in St Mark's Church, Winshill, where he lies next to his wife Eleanor May, is maintained by the Victoria Cross Trust. In addition, the headquarters of the Defence Medical Services is called Coltman House, in his honour, and there is a monument to Bill in the Memorial Gardens in Burton-on-Trent. But perhaps the most appropriate legacy for a man who was a pacifist at heart is the Coltman VC Peace Wood, in Winshill, Staffordshire. He once expressed the hope that there would come a time when it would not be necessary for Victoria Crosses to be won. Well said, Bill!

FIFTEEN

TILL CASH US DO PART

"My wife is an angel," said one man to another he had just met in a pub. *"You're lucky*, mine's still alive!" came the reply. An old joke, but pertinent to this story. At least, that's my excuse for including it here. To even things up gender wise, one of the oldest jokes in the English language goes something like this: husband to wife, "Why do you hate me?" Wife to husband, "Because you love me." Ouch! So, what do you do when the love that once burned so passionately is replaced with a deep loathing for your spouse? Divorce, I hear you cry. Well yes, that's what happens nowadays, but there was a time when things were just not that simple.

In eighteenth-century England, obtaining a divorce was difficult and expensive. Prior to the passing of the Matrimonial Causes Act 1857, a divorce could only be obtained through a private Act of Parliament. Effectively, this meant that each and every divorce required its own piece of legislation. As you can

*Domestic
disharmony*

imagine, the legal process was tortuous, and the cost was estimated to be around £15,000 in today's money, well beyond the reach of the average couple at that time.

Falling out of love, however, was not just the preserve of the well-to-do. A practical solution was needed for couples of more modest means who could no longer stand the sight of one another. Hence, from the 1730s onwards, cases of wife selling began to be recorded. Yes, that's right. Husbands actually started selling their wives! Although not exactly legal (the practice was never enshrined in law), the authorities nevertheless realised that such transactions solved a prickly problem and so turned a blind eye to the process.

Unbelievably, wives were brought to market like cattle, often with a rope around their necks. They would then be required to stand on an auction block while their husbands took bids from the assembled crowd. In 1733, Samuel Whitehouse sold his wife, Mary, at a market in Birmingham for one guinea (a sum equivalent to one pound and one shilling) to Thomas Griffiths, the latter being obliged to take Mary "with all her faults". Some transactions even involved goods being traded, as well as, or instead of, money. One wife was sold for one shilling and sixpence plus a quart of ale, and another for a full barrel of beer!

Do not be fooled, however, into thinking that the practice of wife selling was always a male-dominated process. Sufficient examples exist to suggest that wives were sometimes the instigator of the proposed transaction. When a husband tried to welsh on a deal in Wenlock in 1830, his wife is reported to have said: "Let be, yer rogue! I wull be sold. I wants a change." However, it is generally believed that most wife sales took place with both husband and wife in agreement over the proposed course of action.

A wife auction in progress

In fact, the process of selling a wife could result in the resolution of potential difficulties on both sides of a failing relationship. In cases where a wife was involved in an extramarital affair, for example, a husband was entitled to sue his wife's lover for damaging his property! In selling that 'property' to her lover, the husband would absolve himself of any ongoing responsibility for his wife, and the purchaser would avoid potentially damaging legal action. Presumably the asset in question – or wife – would also have been happy with the outcome, as it has to be surmised that her preference would have been for her boyfriend over her husband.

An example that may well illustrate this point also appears to suggest that the better-off were equally keen to get in on the act. In July 1815, a wife arrived by coach at Smithfield Market in London, whereupon she was sold for the grand sum of 50 guineas and a horse. She promptly left in a smart carriage that had seemingly been waiting for her!

Unfortunately, not all transactions went as smoothly. In Manchester, in 1824, bidding closed at 5 shillings, but as the wife did not like the look of her purchaser she refused to be sold. She was put up for sale again, and this time went for 3 shillings and a quart of ale – to a better-looking bidder, one presumes! Nor were such transactions necessarily permanent. In 1826, William Kaye bought John Turton's wife, Mary, for 5 shillings. Sadly for William, and somewhat suspiciously, he did not last long, and soon shuffled off his mortal coil. Mary promptly returned to John, and they remained together for the next 30 years.

Wife selling even found its way into popular literature. The plot of Thomas Hardy's *The Mayor of Casterbridge,* published in 1886, entailed the main character getting drunk and selling his wife to a sailor, a deed he regrets for the rest of his life.

Amazingly, the custom of wife selling seems to have continued right up until the early years of the twentieth century. British politician James Bryce, writing in 1901, stated: "Everybody has heard of the odd habit of selling a wife, which still occasionally recurs among the humbler classes in England." The last reported case of a wife sale is believed to be that recorded in Yorkshire court records in 1913, where a woman gave evidence to the effect that her husband had sold her to one of his workmates for £1. I suppose the modern equivalent of this bizarre practice would be listing your partner on eBay… erm… spouseBay. Now, there's a thought. "Honey, smile for the camera!"

Thomas Hardy

SIXTEEN

THE NICE HERR GOERING

Just over 70 years after his death, the name Hermann Goering (1893–1946) is still sadly familiar to most of us. A leading member of the Nazi Party, he founded the dreaded German secret police known as 'the Gestapo' and was appointed Commander in Chief of the Luftwaffe, Germany's Air Force, from 1935 until the last days of World War II. However, his infamy stems from his involvement in the establishment of concentration camps and the extermination of approximately six million Jews throughout the duration of World War II.

As a young man, Goering served with distinction as a fighter pilot during World War I. By the time hostilities were renewed in 1939, however, he was addicted to morphine and had become seriously overweight. Following the surrender of Nazi Germany in 1945, Goering was found guilty of war crimes, and crimes against humanity, at the Nuremberg Trials.

*Hermann
Goering*

He was sentenced to death by hanging. His request to be executed as a soldier by firing squad, instead of being strung up as a common criminal, was refused. However, Goering cheated the hangman's noose by committing suicide the night before his planned execution, by way of a capsule of potassium cyanide. Along with Adolf Hitler and other senior Nazis, he was surely one of the twentieth century's most heinous individuals.

But enough of the corpulent, drug-addled mass murderer. I want to tell you about a very different kind of man indeed. Albert Goering (1895–1966) might have been the younger brother of the loathsome Nazi but, as human beings go, he was worlds apart.

Unlike his brother, Albert was a man of profound moral conviction. He was quick to recognise Nazism for what it was and wasn't afraid to speak out against Adolf Hitler and the inhumanity of his policies. Unable to coexist with a regime he found abhorrent, Albert decided to cross the border and set up home in Austria. Unfortunately for him, his new halcyon life was short-lived because Austria was annexed to Nazi Germany in March 1938. As an outspoken opponent of the regime, he was at grave risk of the extreme brutality of the Gestapo, but brotherly love won out and he was protected by Hermann.

It soon became apparent that Nazi anti-Semitism was escalating into a plan for the total extermination of Jews, so Albert took the courageous decision to actively help people escape whenever he could. Many Jews were able to leave Vienna thanks to travel documents and passports procured by Albert. He was even able to help those beyond his immediate field of influence, through his family connection. On many occasions he approached his elder brother, beseeching him to intervene on behalf of individuals who had already been interned in concentration camps.

Hermann, it seems, almost always acquiesced to his brother's requests. Approximately 100 people were freed from concentration camps as a result of Albert's involvement. Contemporary accounts suggest that Albert knew that by massaging his brother's ego he could get him to sign release papers. As one might have expected, it doesn't seem as though the freeing of Jewish prisoners was any kind of humanitarian gesture on behalf of the elder Goering. It would appear instead that these acts of clemency were simply a demonstration to his sibling of his power and influence.

His job as export director at the arms factory, Skoda, often brought Albert into direct contact with Nazi officers. When greeted with the Nazi salute, he always refused to reciprocate, an inaction deemed insulting by Nazis and punishable by imprisonment. On one occasion, a high-ranking SS officer arrived and entered his office unannounced. Albert ordered him to wait outside, and instead asked his assistant, Karel Sobota, to step into the room. They spent the next 30 to 40 minutes casually looking through his family picture albums, before Albert begrudgingly allowed the officer to enter. On another occasion, when recognised by two Nazi officers who saluted him with "Heil Hitler", he immediately responded with, "You can kiss my arse!" Unsurprisingly, he was arrested several times by the Gestapo but was always released through his brother's intervention.

Another act of kindness and solidarity occurred when Albert chanced upon a group of Jews who had been ordered by the Nazis to scrub the pavement on their hands and knees as an act of public humiliation. Survivors recall that he simply removed his jacket, got down on his own knees and began scrubbing the pavement alongside them. The attendant Nazis, aware of his identity, immediately put a stop to the proceedings lest they caused embarrassment to their obese overlord.

Shortly before he committed suicide, Hermann wrote to Albert imploring him to take care of his wife, Emmy, and daughter, Edda. Perversely, Albert was himself imprisoned for several years after the war simply for being the brother of a prominent Nazi. Upon his release, Albert found himself virtually unemployable for the same reason. Fortunately, grateful survivors, whom he had helped to escape, rallied round and supported him during his jobless years. He eventually found work as a designer for a construction firm in Munich.

One final act of benevolence occurred when Albert was on his deathbed. His housekeeper was a woman of modest means, so he married her in order that she would receive his pension as his widow. He died in 1966 at the age of 71.

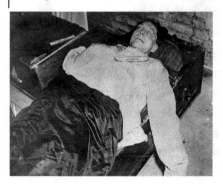

The body of Hermann Goering

The last word is best left to Tatiana Guliaeff, who was just six years old when Albert helped her family to escape from

Vienna with false papers. Upon learning that he had passed away, she wrote him a posthumous letter, which concluded: "Truly we were blessed to have had you in our lives. God rest your soul, my dearly beloved godfather, my Uncle Bear."

SEVENTEEN

THE COPPER SCROLL TREASURE

Most of us today are familiar with what have become collectively known as the 'Dead Sea scrolls'. Discovered between 1946 and 1956, in caves located just over one mile inland from the shore of the Dead Sea, in the modern-day Palestinian territory of the West Bank, the scrolls are of great religious and historical importance. Roughly 40% of them are copies of texts from Hebrew scripture. Some 30% are texts that do not appear in the Hebrew Bible – for example, the Book of Enoch, the Book of Tobit and Psalms 152–155 – and the remainder are manuscripts that relate to particular Jewish sects, which mostly detail beliefs and rules.

However, what is less well known is that one of the scrolls is unique, in that it is made of copper; all of the other scrolls were written on either parchment or papyrus. In addition, the copper scroll differs from the others in terms of its style, script, language and content.

So much so, in fact, that it is thought to have been placed in the cave at a different time to the rest of the scrolls.

The copper scroll was found on 14 March 1952, at the back of Cave No. 3, and has been dated to between 25 CE and 100 CE, making it almost 2,000 years old. What has fascinated archaeologists and treasure hunters alike, however, is the information

The caves in which the scrolls were found

it contains. The scroll could not be unravelled like a parchment, and so, in 1955, it was cut into 23 strips and reassembled. It was then possible to transcribe the Hebrew text. What became apparent was that this scroll was not a literary work, like the others, but a list. And what a list it turned out to be!

The document listed directions to 64 locations where vast quantities of treasure had been hidden. Most of the locations were described as having large deposits of silver and gold secreted there, and the total inventory of the scroll would exceed 1 billion dollars at current values. The locations are quite specific, and presumably would have been well known to those contemporaneous with the production of the scroll. The following is an example of its contents:

A section of the copper scroll

"Forty-two talents lie under the stairs in the salt pit... Sixty-five bars of gold lie on the third terrace in the cave of the old Washers House... Seventy talents of silver are enclosed in wooden vessels that are in the cistern of a burial chamber in Matia's courtyard. Fifteen cubits from the front of the eastern gates, lies a cistern. The ten talents lie in the canal of the cistern… Six silver bars are located at the sharp edge of the rock which is under the eastern wall in the cistern. The cistern's entrance is under the large paving stone threshold. Dig down four cubits in the northern corner of the pool that is east of Kohlit. There will be twenty-two talents of silver coins."

Now, before you start making travel arrangements, let us consider the difficulties of a twenty-first-century treasure seeker. The scroll was produced in copper, presumably to aid its longevity. However, the locations given assume a knowledge of long-gone points of reference. If I were writing an explanation of where I had hidden something, specifically intended for interpretation in hundreds or thousands of years' time, it wouldn't be much use saying: "I hid it under the stairs!" And yet this is precisely what the author has done in this case.

Much has been written about who hid the treasure, although, because it's all pure conjecture, there is little point dwelling for too long on the subject. Suffice it to say that it is likely that the treasure came from either the First Jewish Temple, destroyed by Nebuchadnezzar, King of Babylon, or the Second Jewish Temple, that fell to the Romans.

More pertinent to many today, however, is the question of where it is now. Without being able to identify any of the locations in the modern landscape, the task is a challenging one, to say the least. Also, when one takes into account the fact that the treasure may have been looted, by either the Babylonians or the Romans, the chances of finding a valuable hoard of silver and gold seem somewhat remote. Nonetheless, there are those who, for academic or financial reasons, seem prepared to have a go at finding it.

An extensive search took place in 1962, without success. Many potential locations were excavated, but nothing was found. Subsequent searches have proved equally fruitless, although a few individuals have claimed to have made some minor finds by using the scroll as a guide. However, considering that the site is of great antiquity, the likelihood of discovering small finds when carrying out excavations must be quite high, and so to attribute such discoveries to the directions contained in the copper scroll requires something of a leap of faith.

But don't let me put you off. If you fancy yourself as something of an Indiana Jones, you know where to go. Just remember your hat and sunscreen; it gets very hot down by the Dead Sea!

EIGHTEEN

MARK TWAIN: HERO OF THE AMERICAN CIVIL WAR?

Samuel Langhorne Clemens was born on 30 November 1835 in Florida. No, not the southern US state; this Florida is a village in the US state of Missouri. Never a large village, the population, according to the 2000 United States Census, was a whopping nine residents!

At 13 years of age, Samuel became a printer's apprentice, but by 1858 had switched professions and was a licensed river pilot. However, when Civil War broke out in 1861, river trade drew to a standstill, so Samuel started writing for newspapers. He began to gain notoriety as a writer and would eventually complete 28 books, including *The Adventures of Tom Sawyer*, published in 1869, and *The Adventures of Huckleberry Finn*, in 1885. Yes, Samuel Clemens wrote under the pseudonym 'Mark Twain', which was actually a term he would have used as a river pilot. Apparently, to river pilots, 'mark twain' means two fathoms, or a safe depth for navigation.

During the Civil War, Mark, as I will now refer to him, briefly fought on the side of the Confederates. Years later, in 1887, he was invited to a reunion of Union veterans in Baltimore to explain why he left the American Civil War after just two weeks' service in 1861. The former Confederate gave the following brilliant account of his decision to withdraw.

Mark Twain, sporting his trademark moustache

"When your secretary invited me to this reunion of the Union veterans of Maryland he requested me to come prepared to clear up a matter which he said had long been a subject of dispute and bad blood in war circles in this country – to wit, the true dimensions of my military services in the Civil War, and the effect they had upon the general result. I recognise the importance of this thing to history, and I have come prepared. Here are the details.

I was in the Civil War two weeks. In that brief time, I rose from private to second lieutenant. The monumental feature of my campaign was the one battle which my command fought – it was in the summer of '61. If I do say it, it was the bloodiest battle ever fought in human history; there is nothing approaching it for destruction of human life in the field, if you take into consideration the forces engaged and the proportion of death to survival. And yet you do not even know the name of that battle. Neither do I. It had a name, but I have forgotten it. It is no use to keep private information which you can't show off. In our battle, there were just 15 men engaged on our side – all brigadier-generals but me, and I was a second-lieutenant. On the other side, there was one man. He was a stranger. We killed him. It was night, and we thought it was an army of observation; he looked like an army of observation – in fact, he looked bigger than an army of observation would in the day time; and some of us believed he was trying to surround us, and some thought he was going to turn our position, and so we shot him.

Poor fellow, he probably wasn't an army of observation after all, but that wasn't our fault; as I say, he had all the look of it in the dim light. It was a sorrowful circumstance, but he took the chances of war, and he drew the wrong card; he over-estimated his fighting strength, and he suffered the likely result; but he fell as the brave should fall – with his face to the front and feet to the field – so we buried him with the honours of war, and took his things.

So began and ended the only battle in the history of the world where the opposing force was utterly exterminated, swept from the face of the earth – to the last man. And yet you don't know the name of that battle; you don't even know the name of that man.

Now, then, for the argument. Suppose I had continued in the war, and gone on as I began, and exterminated the opposing forces every time – every two weeks – where would your war have been? Why, you see yourself, the conflict would have been too one-sided. There was but one honourable course for me to pursue, and I pursued it. I withdrew to private life, and gave the Union cause a chance. There, now, you have the whole thing in a nutshell; it was not my presence in the Civil War that determined that tremendous contest – it was my retirement from it that brought the crash. It left the Confederate side too weak."

After his brief but eventful military career, Mark Twain's light shone brightly. He became famous the world over and was acquainted with presidents, artists, scientists, and even European royalty. So well-known was he that fan mail addressed to 'Mark Twain, God knows where', and 'Mark Twain. Somewhere (Try Satan)', duly landed on his doormat.

In his later years

In 1909, he said: "I came in with Halley's Comet in 1835. It is coming again next year, and I expect to go out with it. It will be the greatest disappointment of my life if I don't go out with Halley's Comet. The Almighty has said, no doubt: 'Now here are these two unaccountable freaks; they came in together, they must go out together.'"

Mark Twain died of a heart attack on 21 April 1910, one day after the comet's closest approach to earth!

NINETEEN

THE WORLD'S
WORST POET

If you are familiar with the work of William Topaz McGonagall, I apologise for reminding you about it. If not, then read on, and prepare to be amazed by the sheer inability of the man. As a poet he is unequalled. His work is so bad that it has become legendary, and he has achieved a degree of posthumous fame as a result.

McGonagall was born in Edinburgh, Scotland. For reasons best known to himself, at times he gave his year of birth as 1825 and on other occasions as 1830. What we do know for certain is that he died on 29 September 1902. Not much he could have done to alter that one after the event!

The first 47 – or 52 – years of his life were unremarkable. Like his father before him, William was a handloom weaver, and was married, with seven children. There was little to suggest that he was destined for immortality, except perhaps for his performance in the title role of an amateur production of *Macbeth*. Reaching the point in the play where Macbeth was supposed to die, McGonagall became convinced that the actor playing Macduff was trying to upstage him, and so he refused to succumb! This event is noteworthy because it hints at a degree of misplaced self-confidence, which is a factor that would come to be a trademark of his later life. Other than this example of apparent thespian anarchy, however, nothing remarkable seems to have occurred in the existence of the lowly hand weaver, who was struggling to make a living in the face of increased mechanisation.

All that was to change one day in 1877, when William Topaz McGonagall experienced what can only be described as a 'Road to Damascus' moment. He claimed that a strange kind of feeling came over him, instilling in him a strong desire to write poetry. He later wrote: *"The most startling incident in my life was the time I discovered myself to be a poet, which was in the year 1877."* Oh, how we beg to differ!

His first effort was entitled *An Address to the Rev. George Gilfillan*. It went like this:

Rev. George Gilfillan of Dundee
There is none can you excel.
You have boldly rejected the Confession of Faith,
And defended your cause right well.
The first time I heard him speak,
'Twas in the Kinnaird Hall,
Lecturing on the Garibaldi movement,
As loud as he could bawl.
He is a liberal gentleman,
To the poor while in distress;

And for his kindness to them,
The lord will surely bless.
My blessing on his noble form,
And on his lofty head;
May all good angels guard him while living,
And hereafter when he's dead.

Truly appalling stuff, I think you'll agree. The trouble was, Reverend Gilfillan seemed to like it, although his comment, "Shakespeare never wrote anything like this", might have been shaded in irony.

McGonagall's most famous work was without doubt the *Tay Bridge Disaster*. It recounted a fatal accident that occurred on 28 December 1879, when the rail bridge crossing the River Tay collapsed while a train was passing over it. Owing to its length, I have chosen to reproduce just the very worst bits for your delectation:

Reverend George Gilfillan (1813–1878). In addition to his ministerial duties, Gilfillan was also a poet in his own right.

Beautiful Railway Bridge of the Silv'ry Tay,
Alas! I am very sorry to say
That ninety lives have been taken away
On the last Sabbath day of 1879,
Which will be remembered for a very long time.
I must now conclude my lay
By telling the world fearlessly without the least dismay
That your central girders would not have given way,
At least many sensible men do say,
Had they been supported on each side with buttresses,
At least many sensible men confess,
For the stronger we our houses do build,
The less chance we have of being killed.

As you can see, his work does not scan properly, and the rhymes are terrible. The reason why McGonagall is remembered today is because his work is so bad it takes on a unique and amusing quality, especially when you consider that he saw himself as a serious poet and used to complain bitterly at the abuse he and his work

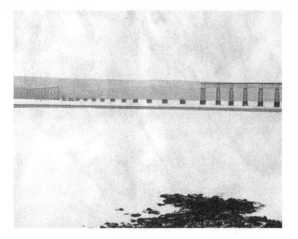

*Tay Bridge
collapse, 1879*

89

received. At public performances he was frequently pelted with eggs, fruit and vegetables. He once complained that he disliked publicans because it was a publican who was the first to throw a plate of peas at him. This suggests that plates of peas were, thereafter, often sent flying in his direction! In 1887, he sailed to New York, hoping that American audiences would be more appreciative of his talents. They were not! Here is an excerpt from his poem entitled *Jottings of New York*:

> Oh mighty city of New York! you are wonderful to
>   behold,
> Your buildings are magnificent, the truth be it told,
> They were the only things that seemed to arrest my eye,
> Because many of them are thirteen storeys high.

Sadly, McGonagall died a poor man and was buried in an unmarked grave in an Edinburgh cemetery; sad because, awful though his poetry is, it became popular after his death, although I'm not sure he would have appreciated the reason for its popularity.

*William
McGonagall
getting ready
to duck?*

TWENTY

LORD LOINCLOTH AND THE RUMBLE IN THE JUNGLE

Long before Muhammad Ali and George Foreman squared up to each other in a boxing ring in Kinshasa, Zaire, on 30 October 1974, in a fight that would become known as 'The Rumble in the Jungle', an altogether different kind of altercation took place in the jungles of East Africa during World War I: a naval battle!

When the subject of World War I is brought to mind, most people, like myself, will conjure up images of muddy trenches, or massive iron-clad battleships blasting away at each other mid Atlantic. However, this particular naval engagement took place on a lake. Yes, all right, Lake Tanganyika is the second deepest lake in the world and covers almost 33,000 square kilometres, but it is just a lake… if a very big one.

Our story begins in 1915 and concerns the Allied colonies of British East Africa and the Belgian Congo

Lake Tanganyika

on the one hand, and the colony of German East Africa on the other. Of massive strategic importance to the protagonists in the war in Africa was Lake Tanganyika, bordering as it did both the German and Belgian territories. Put simply, whoever had control of the lake would also have control of the land surrounding it.

The trouble for the Allies was that Germany was in complete control of it. Captain Gustav Zimmer had two reasonably well-armed riverboats, the *Hedwig von Wissmann* and the *Kingani,* and 150 marines at his disposal. In addition, a larger gunboat called the *Graf von Goetzen* was under construction and would soon be a welcome addition to the captain's modest fleet. Understandably, the British were more than a little keen to reverse this situation, but there was a problem: they didn't have any boats!

Furthermore, gaining access to the lake via the Allied territories was extremely problematic, necessitating the navigation of swamps, jungles and mountain ranges, without roads or railroads to expedite matters. Undeterred by these seemingly insurmountable obstacles, Mr John Lee, an English big-game hunter, approached the British Admiralty in Whitehall, London, with an ambitious – if not hare-brained – plan. He proposed that the Navy dismantle two of its fast river gunboats and ship them to South Africa; at that time an Ally of the British. Once there, they could be transported by rail until the tracks ran out, after which the plan was to cut a path through the jungle and, with the help of some 2,000 natives, essentially carry the dismantled gunboats through jungle, swamp and over mountainous terrain, before eventually descending to the shores of Lake Tanganyika where they could be reassembled and launched.

Most of the naval hierarchy thought Lee was unhinged but they were unable to come up with an alternative proposal and so gave the mission the go-ahead. After all, the disappearance of two small riverboats would hardly be noticed, given the huge losses being sustained in the battle for the Atlantic! The only remaining issue was to appoint someone to lead the expedition. John Lee's only area of expertise was shooting wild animals and, because he had no previous naval experience, he was quickly ruled out of the running.

Instead, the man chosen to undertake the absurd task was Captain Geoffrey Spicer-Simson, a hitherto undistinguished naval officer, whose only previous experience in the command of vessels had resulted in one collision and a direct hit from a torpedo in broad daylight. Unsurprisingly, he had subsequently been assigned to desk duties, and so his appointment to head up the Lake Tanganyika mission was unexpected, to say the least. Presumably, the thinking behind the appointment was that, as the enterprise was almost certainly doomed to fail there was little point in committing someone valuable to it!

And so it was that, on 15 June 1915, the 'Naval Africa Expedition' set sail from England aboard a freighter bound for Cape Town, South Africa. During the voyage,

Captain Geoffrey Spicer-Simson

Spicer-Simson began displaying certain eccentricities. He ordered the ship to display the flag of a rear admiral, despite the fact that there was no one of that seniority on board, and he instructed his subordinates to address him as 'mon colonel'. He claimed to have hunted lions in the Gambia – presumably unaware that lions were not native to that part of Africa – and also gave a detailed account of how he had sunk a German U-boat while in command of a destroyer, which was not true. He also named the gunboats that were being transported 'HMS *Dog*' and 'HMS *Cat*', although he was quickly advised by the Admiralty that they were not suitable names for vessels of the Royal Navy. He eventually settled for *Mimi* and *Toutou* instead.

By the time the expedition reached the Belgian Congo, Spicer-Simson was becoming even more eccentric. He took to wearing a khaki skirt and began tattooing himself. Most bizarre of all, however, was his twice-weekly naked ceremonial bath, that he insisted on taking in the middle of wherever they were camping. It was this unusual bathing ritual that led the African natives to award him the moniker of 'Lord Loincloth'. However, despite the incredibly harsh terrain, and regardless of the odd behaviour of its leader, the party was making excellent progress and, on 28 October 1915, the unbelievable happened. After a journey of 6,000 miles by sea, and another 3,000 miles by land, they reached the Belgian Congo village of Kalemie, on the shore of Lake Tanganyika. An astonishing achievement!

With the gunboats reassembled, Spicer-Simson and his 26 heroic – but slightly bemused – sailors were soon ready for action. Captain Zimmer, by now aware that a British expeditionary force had arrived at the lake, made the logical assumption that they were a purely land-based force, and so dispatched his riverboat *Kingani* to take a few potshots at the sitting ducks. Calmly finishing a prayer meeting, Spicer-Simson sent *Mimi* and *Toutou* to meet the German vessel, which they quickly put out of action with a shot to the wheelhouse, killing the officer in charge in the process. In total, the Germans suffered 3 fatalities and 11 sailors were taken prisoner but, of greater strategic importance, the *Kingani* was captured, renamed HMS *Fifi* and assimilated into the now burgeoning British fleet.

Meanwhile, assuming that his boat had been sunk, and surmising that it must have been hit with shore-based weaponry, Zimmer next sent the *Hedwig von Wissmann* on a reconnaissance mission in order to establish the strength of the British ground force. Spicer-Simson immediately ordered *Mimi* and *Fifi* into the attack, and the *Wissmann* was soon on her way to the bottom of the lake.

By the time the *Graf von Goetzen* was ready for deployment, Belgian forces were rapidly advancing towards Zimmer's base at the port of Kigoma, and a small squadron of Royal Navy seaplanes had made their way to the lake. Now under threat from land, sea and air, Zimmer realised that the situation was hopeless, and so, in July 1916, he ordered the *Goetzen* to be scuttled in shallow water. In a complete reversal, Lake Tanganyika, and as a consequence all of East Africa, was now under British control.

Spicer-Simson had gone from undistinguished pen-pusher to war hero and was duly awarded the

Distinguished Service Order. Following the Battle of Lake Tanganyika, the unconventional captain simply returned to the relative obscurity of his desk job and never saw action again. Geoffrey Spicer-Simson died on 29 January 1947, aged 71.

That is not quite the end of the story, though. In 1924, the *Graf von Goetzen* was salvaged. The *Liemba*, as she is now known, is a passenger and cargo ferry that still runs along the eastern shore of Lake Tanganyika. Additionally, she is believed to have been the inspiration behind C. S. Forester's novel *The African Queen*, and the subsequent film of the same name starring Katharine Hepburn and Humphrey Bogart.

MV *Liemba*

TWENTY-ONE

THE PHANTOM DOGGIE OF LOGIERAIT PARISH

This story about a ghost dog begins not with the birth of a puppy, as one might expect, but with the arrival of a bouncing baby boy. Robert, the latest addition to the Steuart clan, was born on 7 January 1804, less than two years before the family completed the construction of Ballechin House, their brand-new large family home on the Ballechin Estate in the parish of Logierait, Perthshire, Scotland.

In 1825, Robert Steuart elected to pursue a military career in India, serving with the East India Company, where he remained for the next quarter of a century. When he eventually returned home in 1850, Major Steuart, as he now was, took charge of the family estate, which he had inherited in his absence some 16 years earlier.

The major quickly gained a reputation as something of an eccentric, preferring the company of dogs over humans. Apart from Steuart, and his housekeeper Sarah, the only other occupants of Ballechin House were dogs: up to 14 of them at any one time. Always a religious man, Steuart had, during his time in India, incorporated certain aspects of Eastern belief systems into his theology; chief among these was his conviction concerning the concept of transmigration of the soul: the notion that the soul can pass, after death, into another body. In this particular case, Major Steuart announced that after his death his soul would return to occupy the body of his favourite dog: a black spaniel, whose name is unfortunately not recorded. The day in question turned out to be 8 April 1876, when Major Robert Hope Steuart passed away at the age of 72. As the major hadn't married, and was childless, the estate passed to his nephew, one John Skinner.

Skinner was not keen to share his new inheritance with his predecessor, even if the major was now a hairy quadruped who liked to pee on lampposts, so he gave instructions that all dogs on the estate were to be shot. It seems the poor old major was only just getting used to his new poochy existence when he suddenly found himself being blasted back into the afterlife with a shotgun!

However, if Skinner thought that this would be the end of the matter, he was very much mistaken. It would appear that the major, miffed at having died twice in such quick succession, determined instead to haunt his former home in the form of his last incarnation.

The first sign that things weren't quite right came when Skinner's wife was working in the study at Ballechin and noticed a strong smell of dog. Moving across the room to open a window to let out the doggie odour, she felt a nudge on her leg, followed by the sensation of a dog rubbing against her. However, upon looking down, there was no animal to be seen.

On another occasion, a house guest, who coincidentally had a black spaniel of his own, thought he saw it dash across the room. Just as he was thinking that it actually looked a bit too big to be his dog, his own dog suddenly rushed into the room in pursuit of the first animal, who was by now nowhere to be seen. On making enquiries, he was advised that his was the only dog on the premises.

Major Steuart?

It became a common occurrence for guests to be rubbed against and snuffled by an invisible dog, and the sound of a wagging tail banging against doors and furniture was frequently heard. At least it seems the major was in a good mood!

Visiting dogs were often transfixed by the movement of something invisible to the human eye. However, possibly the most unnerving experience occurred with a lady whose pet dog was sleeping on her bed. Awakened by the dog's frightened whimpering, she followed its gaze, only to be met by the sight of two disembodied black paws placed on the bedside table!

Strangely, the spooky hound appears to have acted as a catalyst (or should that be a dogalyst?) for a rapid increase in otherworldly phenomena at the house. A ghost in a silk dress was sighted, bedclothes were pulled off startled sleepers, limping footsteps were often heard, as were sounds of knocking, and what appeared to be a ghostly couple having a row!

John Skinner died in 1895 after being run over by a cab while on a visit to London. The house was subsequently leased to the family of an army captain, with one year's rent having been paid in advance. However, the captain and his family lasted just 11 weeks in the house before being driven out by the spooky goings-on. Ballechin House was by now gaining a reputation among researchers of psychic phenomena as a hotbed of paranormal activity, and it was no surprise, therefore, when two psychic investigators – a Colonel Lemesurier Taylor and a Miss Goodrich-Speer – duly arrived to carry out an investigation. They reported encountering a plethora of psychic phenomena, including loud clanging noises, muffled voices, footsteps from empty rooms, the sound of something heavy being dragged across the floor, a gunshot, and even the sound of a priest conducting a service. Oddly, though, they did not record a single dog-related encounter.

Sadly, the house eventually fell into disrepair and by the early 1930s was no longer suitable for habitation. It remained empty, of humans that is, until finally being demolished in 1963. Modern-day ghost hunters can still visit the area, although I'm not sure how you go about tracking down a phantom dog. You could try throwing a stick and shouting "Fetch!" And should the stick be brought back by an unseen snout, "Good boy, Major!"

TWENTY-TWO

WAS LORD HAW-HAW A TRAITOR?

William Brooke Joyce was born on 24 April 1906 into an Irish Catholic family in Brooklyn, New York, USA. A few years after his birth, the family returned to Ireland permanently, setting up home in Salthill, Galway. After leaving school, William crossed the Irish Sea to England to study at Birkbeck College at the University of London, where he entered the Officer Training Corps. He gained a first-class honours degree, but also an interest in Fascism.

On 22 October 1924, Joyce was acting as a steward at a meeting supporting a Conservative Party candidate in the forthcoming general election when he was set upon by a group of Communists, resulting in him being slashed across the face with a razor. He was left with a permanent scar across his right cheek, from his ear to the corner of his mouth. Even at this young age he was an anti-Semite, claiming that his attackers were Jews.

By 1932, Joyce had joined the British Union of Fascists (BUF), led by Sir Oswald Mosley. He was soon appointed to the position of Director of Propaganda and was an eager participant in violent confrontations with anti-Fascists. However, he eventually fell out with the BUF over a number of policy issues, including his own fervent anti-Semitism. He was eventually dismissed from the organisation after the 1937 elections, following which he formed his own political party: the National Socialist League.

By 1939, with war clouds gathering, Joyce fled with his wife to Germany. The British Government had passed a new defence law permitting the detention of suspected Nazi sympathisers, and it had become apparent that the authorities in Britain were about to arrest him. William Joyce became a naturalised German citizen in 1940.

Propaganda was an important weapon during World War II, and Japanese, Italian and German broadcasters dedicated significant airtime to transmitting disinformation aimed at weakening the morale of Allied troops and citizens alike. Two of the most famous propagandist broadcasters were Axis Sally and Tokyo Rose but, for British radio listeners, it was the name 'Lord Haw-Haw' that became synonymous with the demoralising transmissions.

The moniker 'Lord Haw-Haw' was initially given to a broadcaster by the name of Wolf Mittler but, after auditioning for the job of announcer for German radio's English service, William Joyce replaced Mittler and made the alias his own. With an upper-class English accent, he always began his broadcasts with the words: "Germany calling, Germany calling, Germany calling."

His messages were frequently sarcastic and menacing, urging the Allies to surrender in the face of Germany's overpowering superiority.

While the British public were discouraged from tuning in to his broadcasts, many did so. At the height of his influence, it is estimated that he was attracting 6 million regular and 18 million occasional listeners. As time went on, Joyce became increasingly confident, even to the point of revealing his true identity on air. However, as the war progressed, and the tide started to turn against Nazi Germany, so his confidence and demoralising influence started to wane.

Millions of Britons listened to Joyce's broadcasts via the wireless radio

Joyce recorded his final broadcast on 30 April 1945, as the battle for Berlin raged. Clearly drunk, it was a rambling affair that concluded with a defiant: "Heil Hitler and farewell." He was captured by British forces on 28 May 1945 near the German border with Denmark. After engaging him in conversation, he was asked whether he was Joyce, whereupon he reached into his pocket. Believing him to be armed, he was shot, sustaining wounds to the buttocks. It transpired that he was actually reaching for a false passport. Joyce was subsequently driven to a border post and handed over to British military police. Taken to London, he was charged with high treason and tried at the Old Bailey.

An injured Joyce, under armed guard, 1945

On 19 September 1945, William Joyce was found guilty of treason and sentenced to death by hanging. He appealed against the sentence, but his conviction was upheld by both the Court of Appeal, on 1 November 1945, and the House of Lords, on 13 December 1945. As he prepared to die, Joyce made the following unrepentant statement:

In death as in life, I defy the Jews who caused this last war, and I defy the power of darkness which they represent. I warn the British people against the crushing imperialism of the Soviet Union. May Britain be great once again, and in the hour of greatest danger in the West, may the standard be raised from the dust, crowned with the words – 'You have conquered nevertheless'. I am proud to die for my ideals and I am sorry for the sons of Britain who have died without knowing why.

William Joyce was executed at Wandsworth Prison on 3 January 1946. He was 39 years old. His remains were buried in an unmarked grave within the walls of the prison. In 1976, his body was exhumed and re-interred in the Protestant section of the New Cemetery in Bohermore, Galway, Ireland.

As a traitor to his country, he surely could not have expected anything less. Except there is a problem: William Joyce was not British! As mentioned above, Joyce was born in the USA, and his father, although

Irish by birth, had become an American citizen in 1894. Joyce himself had taken German citizenship in 1940. So, if during the period that he was broadcasting he was either American or German, how was it that he was convicted by the British judiciary of treason? Surely, to be guilty of treason against Great Britain you have to be British.

The argument put forward by Attorney General Sir Hartley Shawcross, and upon which Joyce was convicted, was tenuous in the extreme. It transpired that, while living in the UK, Joyce had obtained a British passport under false pretences by lying about his country of origin. In normal circumstances, once the deceit had been revealed, the passport would have been declared null and void. However, Shawcross argued that, for so long as the passport was deemed to be valid, Joyce had owed allegiance to the King. Consequently, since he did not take German citizenship until 1940, his early broadcasts, while still in possession of a British passport, were treasonable. It was on this basis that he was convicted and the conviction upheld on appeal.

That Joyce conspired with an enemy of both the UK and the USA is undeniable. However, the USA did not enter World War II until December 1941, by which time he was a German citizen. Presumably, therefore, he could not have been tried for treason by the USA because, for the period of time that he remained an American citizen, Germany was not an enemy of the USA, and by the time hostilities were declared he was German.

It seems likely, therefore, that the decision by the British to prosecute Joyce for treason was based on the fact that it was the only conceivable option available to secure a conviction. Morally speaking, it is probably reasonable to regard William Joyce as a traitor but, from a legal perspective, it is highly questionable whether he should ever have been tried and convicted. So, was Lord Haw-Haw a traitor? What do you think?

TWENTY-THREE

GORDON BENNETT, IT'S SWEET FANNY ADAMS!

English is one of the most widely-spoken languages in the world today. Approximately 360 million people speak it as their first language, and to a staggering half a billion it is their second language. Roughly speaking, English is a blend of the language spoken by the Anglo-Saxons, who invaded England about 1,500 years ago, and a Scandinavian language spoken by Viking invaders, who arrived a couple of hundred years later. However, the English we recognise today did not evolve until around the time of the poet and playwright William Shakespeare (1564–1616); which is fortunate for both his legacy and our culture, although a few schoolchildren may beg to differ!

Between Elizabethan England and the present day, the names of a few people have embedded themselves into the language to such an extent that we use them as expressions today without giving much – if any –

thought as to their origin. Time, I surmised, for me to have a rummage around to see if I could put some flesh on the bones, so to speak.

Let's kick off with 'Gordon Bennett': a mild expletive used to express surprise. James Gordon Bennett Jr was born in 1841, the son of – yes, you've guessed it – James Gordon Bennett (1795–1872). Old man Bennett was the founder, in 1835, of the *New York Herald*, and by 1866 had handed over control of the newspaper to his son. A wealthy young man, Bennett Junior cared little for the opinion of others, especially with regard to his eccentric and often unsociable behaviour. One particular example of his reprehensible conduct occurred at a party held by his fiancée's father in 1877. Being somewhat inebriated and needing to relieve himself, instead of withdrawing to the little boys' room he simply whipped out his 'John Thomas' (more of that later) and urinated into a fireplace in front of the host and his assembled guests. The marriage did not go ahead! Such was his outlandish behaviour that he was eventually obliged to leave the USA altogether, although he continued to run the *New York Herald* from Europe. James Gordon Bennett Jr died in 1918.

James Gordon Bennett Jr (1841–1918)

JAMES GORDON BENNETT
PROPRIETOR AND PUBLISHER
"THE NEW YORK HERALD" AND "EVENING TELEGRAM"

An alternative candidate for the origin of the term 'Gordon Bennett' is Lieutenant General Henry Gordon Bennett (1887–1962), an Australian, who reportedly abandoned his command and fled to safety during the Japanese invasion of Singapore in February 1942, leaving his troops behind to be captured. However, as examples of the expression appear in print prior to World

War II, this seems unlikely in the extreme. The phrase is also what is known as a 'minced oath', whereby it is used in place of a more profane expletive. In this case, Gordon Bennett has replaced 'Cor blimey', which is itself an abbreviated version of 'God blind me'.

Another example of a minced oath is 'Sweet Fanny Adams', an expression used to indicate 'absolutely nothing'. Sadly, this phrase emerged from a tragic event. On 24 August 1867, eight-year-old Fanny Adams was abducted and murdered while out playing near her home in Alton, Hampshire, England. Her murderer was soon arrested and was hanged for the crime.

The case caused nationwide outrage, but it was the macabre humour of the sailors of the British Royal Navy that first resulted in the poor girl's name being subsumed into the English language. Tinned food was at that time the latest method of food preservation and, in 1869, sailors were provided with tins of mutton as part of their shipboard diet. Apparently, the taste was appalling, and sailors soon began to liken the tinned meat to the dead girl's remains. However,

The headstone of Fanny Adams

that is not the meaning of Sweet Fanny Adams that we recognise today. At some indeterminate point, the phrase transformed into a minced oath, used in place of the coarse expletive 'f**k all'.

The saying 'Bob's your uncle', meaning 'everything is fine', has its probable origin in British politics. Prime Minister Viscount Cranborne (1830–1903) also went by the name of Robert Arthur Talbot Gascoyne-Cecil,

*Arthur Balfour
(1848–1930)*

3rd Marquess of Salisbury. Clearly at the front of the queue when names were being handed out, the important bit here is to remember that his first name was Robert. In acts of unbridled nepotism, he frequently promoted his nephew, Arthur Balfour (1848–1930), to various, and increasingly senior, political positions, despite the fact that the lad had previously shown little interest in public office. Arthur eventually became Prime Minister himself! Thus it was commonly inferred that you will be assured an easy life, and a cushy career path, provided Bob's your uncle.

'Hobson's choice' is an expression used to indicate that there is absolutely no choice at all and is one that Shakespeare himself might have been familiar with because it refers to one Thomas Hobson (1544–1631), a contemporary of the great Bard of Avon. Hobson was the proprietor of a carrier and horse rental business in Cambridge, England, who had a very strict policy on renting out his horses. The choice given to his customers was that they were to have the nearest horse or none. In other words: not their choice, but Hobson's choice.

'Happy as Larry' is clearly self-explanatory, but who was Larry and why was he so happy? It seems that the gentleman in question was Larry Foley (1847–1917), a very successful Australian boxer who never lost a fight; he retired at the age of 32, having made his fortune in prize money.

And so, as promised earlier, we finally arrive at 'John Thomas': a euphemism for the male appendage. Sadly, it does not appear that the term refers to any particular individual. Historically, the name 'John' or 'John Thomas' was used colloquially in England to refer to a man from the serving classes, such as a footman or butler. Quite how the name transposed from man to member is, however, unclear. It has been erroneously claimed that the term originally comes from D. H. Lawrence's steamy novel, *Lady Chatterley's Lover*. In fact, the name also appears in an earlier novel by the same author, published in 1927, entitled *John Thomas and Lady Jane*. However, as the use of the term 'John Thomas' to refer to either male servants or their wedding tackle predates the twentieth century, it seems as though Lawrence simply utilised the pre-existing moniker to indicate a person of lower status.

Larry Foley (1847–1917)

TWENTY-FOUR

THE VOYNICH MANUSCRIPT

In 1912, an antiquarian bookseller bought a very old book. Nothing unusual there. After all, booksellers need to buy books in order to be able to sell them! What was unusual about this particular book, however, was that it was, and has remained, completely indecipherable. Wilfrid Voynich, the bookseller in question, opened his first bookshop in London in 1898. Prior to this, he had been a Polish revolutionary. A somewhat seismic career change, I think you'll agree! His life as a dealer in books, however, had been unremarkable; until that is, he came across the codex that would become known as the 'Voynich Manuscript'.

Wilfrid was examining a collection of manuscripts, which he said had been residing undisturbed in a castle in southern Europe, when he came upon the book that was henceforth to bear his name and ensure him a degree of immortality. He later commented:

... my attention was especially drawn by one volume. It was such an ugly duckling compared with the other manuscripts... I found that it was written entirely in cipher... the vellum upon which it was written, the calligraphy, the drawings, and the pigments, suggested to me as the date of its origin the latter part of the thirteenth century...

Wilfrid Voynich (1865–1930)

The fact that this was a thirteenth-century manuscript in cipher convinced me that it must be a work of exceptional importance, and to my knowledge the existence of a manuscript of such an early date written entirely in cipher was unknown, so I included it among the manuscripts which I purchased from this collection... It was not until sometime after the manuscript came into my hands that I read the document bearing the date 1665, which was attached to the front cover... This document, which is a letter from Johannes Marcus Marci to Athanasius Kircher, making a gift of the manuscript to him, is of great significance.

Johannes Marcus Marci was a Bohemian scientist and doctor. The manuscript appears to have come into his possession following the death of Georg Baresch, the previous owner and an antique collector from Prague. Athanasius Kircher was a polymath, who has been compared to Leonardo da Vinci owing to the enormous range of subjects he studied. Earlier in 1639, Baresch had written to Kircher, seeking help in translating a mysterious book illustrated with pictures of stars, plants and chemical secrets that had been written in an

Athanasius Kircher (1602–1680)

unknown script. Kircher was unable to decipher the text but presumably expressed considerable interest in the manuscript because it was eventually gifted to him.

All this is very interesting, but what actually is the Voynich Manuscript? Physically, it is a codex (the earliest form of book, replacing scrolls and wax tablets), and it measures 22.5 centimetres by 16 centimetres and is approximately 5 centimetres thick. It is thought to have originally contained 116 folios, but 14 are missing, leaving us with 102. The writing is elegant, but the script is entirely unknown. Most pages contain illustrations of herbs, constellations and arrangements of tubes for transporting liquid. Small female figures also appear frequently in the manuscript. By interpreting the illustrations, the book appears to be divided into sections of differing subject matter. A herb section depicts known herbs as well as some unknown or imaginary varieties. An astronomical section has images of the sun, moon and stars, as well as symbols of the zodiac. A biological section

Photograph of a section of the Voynich Manuscript

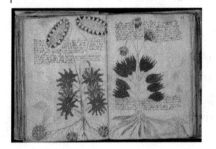

contains what appear to be anatomical illustrations. A pharmaceutical section has depictions of containers alongside herbs. The manuscript also appears to contain a recipe section and a cosmology section.

The intended purpose of the manuscript, however, remains a mystery. A number of suggestions have been put forward to try to put the book into some kind of historical context. Among the most notable are:

- discoveries and inventions by the thirteenth-century friar Roger Bacon, written in a complicated code;
- a book of nonsense written by a medieval quack, to impress potential customers;
- a prayer book from the Cathars which survived the Inquisition, written in some kind of Germanic pidgin; and
- meaningless strands of characters, composed by sixteenth-century occult philosopher, astrologer and alchemist, John Dee, for monetary gain.

In 2009, a piece of parchment from the manuscript was radiocarbon-dated, with a resulting date range suggesting its production to have been between 1404 and 1438, effectively ruling out both Bacon and Dee as potential authors and making Voynich's initial assessment more than 100 years too early. Numerous cryptographers, both amateur and professional, have studied the manuscript, including British and American codebreakers from both world wars, without success. It is generally regarded as being one of the most significant cases in the history of cryptography.

The Voynich Manuscript was purchased in 1961 by the antiquarian book dealer Hans Peter Krauss, for 24,500 dollars. Unable to find a buyer, he donated it to Yale University in 1969, where it remains to this day, unimaginatively registered as 'MS 408'. Voynich himself believed that the book would increase in value once it had been deciphered. However, it is precisely because the Voynich Manuscript remains an enigma that it retains its unique fascination. If the day ever comes when the manuscript is decoded, a little bit of ancient mystification will disappear forever. Historians and cryptographers may beg to differ, but I for one hope that that day never comes.

TWENTY-FIVE

WHO PUT BELLA
IN THE WYCH ELM?

On 18 April 1943, four boys with an interest in ornithology were enthusiastically going about their bird spotting in Hagley Woods, near Birmingham, England, when one of them made a grisly discovery. Climbing a wych elm tree, one of the boys peered inside the hollow trunk and discovered a human skull residing there. Understandably, the youngsters were traumatised by their discovery and decided that the best course of action would be to remain silent on the subject. However, Tommy Willetts, the youngest of the boys, felt the need to unburden himself of this secret, and so he told his father, who immediately notified the police.

Warwickshire police were quickly on the scene and discovered not just a skull but the entire skeleton of a young woman. Well, entire minus one hand, the bones of which were soon found scattered near to the tree.

In addition to the bones, the tree trunk also contained some scraps of clothing, a pair of old shoes and a gold ring. A piece of taffeta had also been stuffed into the mouth of the skull. The pathologist who examined the remains determined that they were of a woman aged about 35, that she was around 5 feet tall with mousy-coloured hair and that she had irregular teeth. He further concluded that the most likely cause of death was asphyxiation, due to the fabric found in the skull's mouth, and that death had occurred approximately 18 months previously. The position in which she was found suggested that she had been placed in the tree trunk shortly after death, as rigor mortis would have prevented the body from being arranged in such a manner.

A description of the woman, based on the pathologist's work and details of the clothing found with the body, produced no leads for the police, nor did a trawl through approximately 3,000 cases of missing persons from around the country. Rumours of a black magic sacrifice began to circulate but, by the end of 1943, and with World War II dominating life in the UK, the body in the tree soon faded from people's memories. That is until the case took a bizarre turn. Graffiti referring to the woman in the woods started to appear. The first said, 'Who Put Lubella Down the Wych Elm?'; and a second read, 'Hagley Wood Bella'. More followed and, while seeming to be the work of one person, eventually the phrase, 'Who Put Bella in the

The skull with hair still attached to the forehead

Wych Elm?', frequently appeared on walls in the West Midlands of England. Was someone trying to tell the authorities something anonymously? If so, they chose a most enigmatic turn of phrase!

Mysterious graffiti

Subsequently, the phrase has appeared on walls and monuments from time to time, occasionally with variant spellings. The last time was as recently as 1999!

As a result of the graffiti, the unidentified woman became known as 'Bella'. With nothing else to go on, even the police adopted the moniker when referring to the case. The identity of Bella, however, remained a complete mystery; until, that is, a journalist by the name of Wilfred Byford-Jones wrote an article about the case for the *Wolverhampton Express and Star* in 1953. Subsequently, Byford-Jones received a letter claiming that the woman in the tree was the Dutch girlfriend of a Nazi agent who had strangled her following an argument.

The letter went on to name the woman as Clarabella Dronkers and stated that she had been in her early thirties at the time of her death. Although the letter was signed only 'Anna', the details given in it ticked several boxes. Her age was about right, and the name was also a match; assuming, of course, that the original graffiti artist knew something about the case. The fact that she was not British could also explain why she wasn't listed as a missing person. Interestingly, records indicate that a Nazi spy by the name of Johannes Marinus Dronkers was executed at Wandsworth Prison on 31 December 1942. Could 'Anna' have simply been unaware that the couple were actually married?

More recently, declassified MI5 files have revealed another candidate for the body in the woods. A Gestapo agent named Josef Jakobs, arrested in 1941, was carrying a photograph of Clara Bauerle, a cabaret singer and German movie actress. Bauerle, whom Jakobs said was his lover, had spent two years working in the music halls of the West Midlands, and spoke English with a Birmingham accent. Consequently, Jakobs said that she'd been recruited as a secret agent by the Nazis and was to have been used in the Midlands area. The name 'Clara Bauerle' does not trip easily off an English tongue, and it seems that she was colloquially known as 'Clarabella' or 'Bella'. Bauerle was born in 1906 – making her the right age for the dead woman – and, more significantly, there are no recordings, film appearances or live performances credited to her after 1941.

Josef Jakobs is known to history as the last person to be executed at the Tower of London. He was shot by a firing squad on 15 August 1941. Could the spy ring Bauerle was involved with have regarded her association with the captured Jakobs as an untenable risk, necessitating her disposal?

Now, I know what you're thinking: this should be an easy one to resolve in the twenty-first century. Simply obtain samples of DNA from living relatives of the two women and compare them to DNA from the remains of the dead woman. There is, however, a problem. The skeletal remains are missing! It seems that after the post-mortem they were passed to a colleague of the pathologist at the University of Birmingham to enable further tests to be carried out, but no records exist of what happened to them after that.

Perhaps, somewhere in the storerooms of the university, there is a box containing old bones, with the name 'Bella' scribbled on it. Or maybe she was quietly laid to rest in a local cemetery. Whatever their current location, if her remains could be found it might be possible to finally reveal the identity of the woman in the tree. However, even if Bella's bones were to be rediscovered after the passage of more than 70 years, the vexing question would still remain: Who put Bella in the wych elm?

TWENTY-SIX

OH, SISTER!

Being the sibling of a famous, or infamous, individual, overshadowed by your more renowned brother or sister, would be a frustrating experience, you might think. That was certainly the case for some of the following sisters of famous historical characters – but not all, it would seem.

Like her brother, Wolfgang Amadeus Mozart, Maria Anna Mozart was a musical genius. Also like her younger brother, she was trained by her father Leopold, a court musician. For many years, the young Maria and Wolfgang toured, playing to audiences of thousands, enthralling them with musical ability seemingly beyond their years. However, upon reaching the age of 18, the career of Maria was brought to an abrupt end by Leopold because it was not deemed appropriate, at that time, for women to tour as musicians.

Nevertheless, Maria does not seem to have been resentful of her brother's success. The siblings retained a strong emotional attachment for one another, and she was deeply affected by his untimely death in 1791, aged just 35. Maria went on to marry and raise a family. She died in 1829 at the age of 78.

Maria and Wolfgang with their father

Unfortunately for Rosalie Poe, sister of famed American writer Edgar Allan Poe, life was not so benevolent. Born around 1810, she was approximately two years younger than her brother, but they were separated as infants because, by 1811, both parents were dead. Unlike her talented brother, Rosalie was described as being hopelessly dull and as having a strange, rather off-putting manner. The two had a distant relationship and, following the early death of Edgar in 1849, Rosalie tried to make a living by selling photographs of her brother, as well as household objects she claimed were once owned by him. In truth, the so-called 'Poe artefacts' had no connection to the writer at all. Unable to support herself, Rosalie was eventually given lodgings in a charity home in Washington, DC, where she died in 1874.

However, the saddest and most tragic of these tales of siblings of the famous must surely be that of Emily and Mary Wilde, half-sisters of the novelist and playwright Oscar Wilde. Their father, Sir William Wilde, was an eminent surgeon, and the girls were the result of an extra-marital affair. Consequently, Sir William went to great lengths to keep their lives a carefully guarded secret. It is not even known whether Oscar ever knew of their existence.

In 1871, Emily and Mary were sent to live with a relative in Monaghan, Ireland, where they attended a welcome ball held in their honour. During a waltz, Emily's crinoline dress swished across an open fire and caught alight. Mary immediately came to her sister's aid but, while trying to beat out the flames, her own dress caught fire. Horrifically burned, both girls succumbed to their injuries; Emily was 24 and Mary 22. A tragedy indeed, but perhaps the saddest part of the story is what happened next. Desperate to avoid adverse publicity, Sir William Wilde used all his influence to ensure that his reputation was not tarnished by the deaths of his illegitimate daughters. At his request, no inquest was held, and the sisters' remains were quietly interred in a local churchyard. Even the name 'Wilde' was altered to 'Wylie' in contemporaneous reports of the accident in order to deflect attention from Sir William. His efforts seem to have been rewarded because the meagre obituary that appeared in newspapers referred to 'the Wylie sisters'.

The sisters of famous aviators, on the other hand, seem to have fared rather well. Katharine Wright, sister of pioneers Wilbur and Orville, handled their business affairs and was the only one of the trio to obtain a college degree. Along with her brothers, she was presented with the prestigious Legion of Honour award by France, remaining one of the few American women to hold the award. However, Katharine sadly died of pneumonia in 1929, aged just 54.

Katharine Wright

Muriel Earhart might not have shared her sister Amelia's love of aviation, but she nevertheless, and possibly as a consequence, enjoyed a very long and active life herself. A schoolteacher by profession, Muriel was also influential in her local community, becoming 'Citizen of the Year' in her hometown of Medford, Massachusetts, in 1979. She also wrote articles and books, including the story of her sister's life and disappearance. Muriel died in 1998 at the age of 98.

The sisters of Nazi Germany's Fuhrer, Adolf Hitler, and his wife, Eva Braun, managed a little better than their infamous siblings. Adolf and Eva committed suicide shortly before the end of World War II, leaving their bereaved sisters, Paula Hitler and Ilse Braun, to face the music, so to speak. Paula had been engaged to a Nazi euthanasia doctor, but the Russians caught up with him before they could marry. Such was the stigma of her surname that she was forced to live in seclusion in a two-roomed flat under the pseudonym 'Paula Wolff'. She died in 1960, aged 64.

Ilse, on the other hand, was careful to distance herself from her sister's Nazi associates. However, being Eva's sister, she was unable to avoid meeting the Fuhrer himself, who she thought looked better in his propaganda portraits. She later became a journalist for a right-wing newspaper, eventually dying of cancer in 1979, aged approximately 70.

That artist Vincent van Gogh suffered with mental health issues is well known; he cut off his own ear and shot himself! Judging from the life of his sister, however, it would appear that the affliction may have been hereditary. Wilhelmina van Gogh was an early feminist, helping to raise funds for the Dutch National Bureau for Women's Work. She herself worked at a hospital. Unfortunately, thereafter things went

Wilhelmina, before the onset of mental illness

*Ama Jetsun
Pema*

rapidly downhill. Aged just 40, she was diagnosed with dementia and placed in psychiatric care. There she remained for another 40 years, sitting in a chair in the lounge, and having to be force fed. With the benefit of hindsight, it would seem that Vincent made the right decision!

Ama Jetsun Pema may not be a name with which you are familiar. No, I wasn't either. Jetsun was born in Tibet in 1940 and spent the first 10 years of her life in her native country, before leaving for India in order to further her education. She completed her studies in England and returned to India in 1964. For 42 years, until her retirement in 2006, Jetsun was President of the Tibetan Children's Villages, a school system for Tibetan refugee students. She was awarded the UNESCO medal in 1999 and is fondly known as the 'Mother of Tibet'. All very well, but who is her famous sibling, you are probably thinking. The clue is in her country of origin. Yes, of course, Jetsun is the sister of the fourteenth, and current, Dalai Lama. Oddly, though, she has only recently begun studying Buddhism!

TWENTY-SEVEN

WHAT'S THAT DOING THERE?

Archaeologists spend a lot of time digging things up (I like, on occasion, to state the obvious!). As the science of archaeology has evolved over the last century, existing techniques have improved and new ones have been developed that enable artefacts to be dated with reasonable accuracy. Dendrochronology can be used to date wood through tree ring analysis; radiocarbon-dating can date an object containing organic material by measuring the amount of radioactive decay; and stratigraphy can date an object by the layer of rock or soil in which it was discovered. In addition, the style or type of an object can be used to date it by comparing it to other known examples.

Occasionally, however, an object turns up for which science can offer no logical explanation. In these cases, rather than being displayed and admired, they tend to be shut away in the storage facilities of museums and universities, in the academic equivalent of the 'too hard basket'. Typically, these are objects or other evidence for human existence that appear to be in a contextually impossible place. In other words, they are found in a stratigraphical layer that pre-dates human existence. The Scottish-born American biologist, Ivan T. Sanderson, proposed the use of the collective term 'Out-of-place Artefacts' (OOPArts), and the phrase is today commonly used to define such items.

While many objects do exist which present no apparent explanation, there are, of course, those artefacts that transpire to be the result of mistaken interpretation, or just a product of plain fabrication. As it is my intention to be as concise as possible, I shall not provide details of objects where a satisfactory explanation has been established. What follows, therefore, are examples of OOPArts that continue to defy rational explanation.

In 1844, quarrymen working near Rutherford in Scotland were stunned to find a piece of gold thread embedded in rock 8 feet below ground level.

In 1851, a clumsy Mr Hiram de Witt dropped a lump of gold-bearing quartz that he had earlier purchased in California. To his surprise, when the rock broke apart, a 2-inch iron nail lay inside it. Apparently, it was straight, had a perfect head and was only slightly corroded. Another nail partly embedded in a piece of stone was reported in 1845. The stone had come from a quarry in Kingoodie, Scotland.

On a cold day in 1891, Mrs Culp, from Morrisonville, Illinois, was breaking coal into manageable-sized lumps when she spotted a chain in the middle of the pile. When she picked it up, she noticed that each end of the chain was firmly embedded in two different lumps of coal. The lumps fitted together perfectly and had been a single piece of coal before Mrs Culp had broken it in two. Coal is formed over deep time and is the result of dead plant matter being crushed and sealed underground. While some coal is thought to be as old as 2 billion years, most is believed to have been laid down between 360 and 300 million years ago, when forests of ferns grew in vast tropical swamps*.

More quarrying, this time in Aix-en-Provence, France, revealed something even more astonishing. Between 1786 and 1788, large quantities of limestone were required for a building project, and quarrying had reached almost 50 feet below ground level. At this level, workmen were flabbergasted to find the stumps of stone pillars. Digging further, they came upon petrified wooden tool handles and some coins. These items were found to be on top of a wooden board several feet long. The board was also petrified, indicating great age. The limestone at this level is 300 million years old!

In 1983, a shocked Professor Amanniyazov reported the discovery of what appeared to be human footprints in Mesozoic strata. As Director of Turkmenistan's Institute of Geology, he was in the process of uncovering more than 1,500 dinosaur tracks when, to his utter disbelief, he came across human-like footprints among those of the dinosaurs. The feet that had left the prints must have passed by at least 150 million years ago.

A skeleton of a modern human, minus head and feet, resides in the British Museum. It is the skeleton of a woman of about 5 feet 2 inches in height. Nothing exceptional about that, except that it was found encased in limestone on the Caribbean island of Guadeloupe. Modern techniques have dated the rock in which she was found to 28 million years ago. The limestone block containing 'Guadeloupe Woman' was put on display at the museum in 1812. Following the publication of Darwin's *On the Origin of Species*, it was removed to the basement, where it currently resides.

So, what does all this mean? Well, we know that our earliest ancestors, Homo erectus, first put in an appearance in Africa between 1 and 2 million years ago, and that we were not capable of making metallic objects at that early stage in our development. The earliest evidence of metalworking by humans is less than 10,000 years old. The earth itself is thought to be about 4.5 billion years old, and the earliest multicellular organisms appeared somewhere in the region of 1.7 billion years ago.

Given our understanding of the process of evolution, it doesn't seem possible that intelligent life could have developed earlier than our own ancestry, although we are dealing with an immense period of time. However, could an entire society really have risen and fallen without leaving a trace on the surface of the planet? Well, yes! If mankind disappeared from the earth tomorrow, it is estimated that all trace of manmade structures would completely vanish within about 50,000 years. Most mainstream scientists, however, dismiss the possibility of another form of intelligent life having developed earlier than modern humankind. They also pour scorn on the suggestion that intelligent life from elsewhere in the universe may have colonised the planet prior to human existence.

What, then, do we make of OOPArts? It seems almost impossible that an earlier civilisation could have inhabited the earth, and yet there they are. Ultimately, your guess is as good as mine. Food for thought, though, don't you think?

TWENTY-EIGHT

STRANGE BUT TRUE!

Every now and then, facts present themselves that, on the face of it, seem unlikely to be true. As a writer on matters of historical interest – or not, as some may argue – I felt obliged to root out the actuality behind some of the more bizarre claims that purport to be historical facts. What follows are examples of improbable statements that turned out to be perfectly accurate observations.

The Roman Empire was formally founded in 27 BCE, in place of the pre-existing Roman Republic; and, believe it or not, was not dissolved until 29 May 1453, when Mehmed the Conqueror captured Constantinople, causing the Roman Empire to finally collapse. The Ottoman Empire was founded in 1299 by Osman I and officially abolished on 1 November 1922 following the Turkish War of Independence. Most scholars agree that Jesus was actually born a few years before the date assigned to his birth by

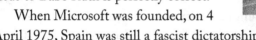

Dionysius Exiguus in the sixth century – somewhere between 6 and 4 BCE seems most probable. What we do know for sure is that American baseball star Babe Ruth was born on 6 February 1895. Thus the statement that two empires spanned the entire gap from Jesus to Babe Ruth is perfectly correct.

Babe Ruth in action

When Microsoft was founded, on 4 April 1975, Spain was still a fascist dictatorship.

Alexander Bain was granted British patent number 9745 on 27 May 1843 for his invention called the 'Electric Printing Telegraph'. We know it better today as the fax machine. Five days earlier, the first major wagon train set out west on the Oregon Trail.

When the pyramids were being built, there were still woolly mammoths, is an implausible-sounding claim. Indeed, we tend to associate the woolly mammoth with our cave-dwelling Neolithic predecessors, the former having been hunted into extinction by the latter. However, the last known population of the elephant's cuddly ancestor died out as recently as 1650 BCE, probably due to a lack of genetic diversity, owing to dwindling numbers.

Woolly mammoth

Pyramid of Djoser

The earliest known Egyptian pyramid, the Pyramid of Djoser, was constructed between 2630 and 2611 BCE. Not only is this statement correct, but it turns out that the pointy mausoleums and shaggy mammals co-existed for almost 1,000 years!

McDonald's was founded in 1940, as a barbecue restaurant, by Richard and Maurice McDonald. A few days later, the first prisoners began to arrive at Auschwitz concentration camp in Poland.

In 1620, when the Pilgrim Fathers arrived in Plymouth, Massachusetts, to set up the first permanent settlement in New England, they faced a tumultuous struggle. By the end of February 1621, approximately half of them were dead due to the cold winter weather and inadequate accommodation. By contrast, the city of Santa Fe, founded by Spanish colonists in 1610, was faring rather better. It is the oldest state capital city in the USA and the oldest city in New Mexico. Santa Fe means 'holy faith' in Spanish. While the Pilgrim Fathers were battling appalling weather, and succumbing to disease and malnutrition, Santa Fe could already boast a hotel and a restaurant! Unfortunately, the hospitality on offer in Santa Fe would have been of little use to the newly arrived settlers because it is well over 2,000 miles from Plymouth, Massachusetts.

Nintendo was founded on 23 September 1889 – initially as a maker of handmade playing cards – less than a year after Jack the Ripper had been stalking his victims in London's notorious East End.

When the Aztec Empire was founded in 1428, the University of Oxford had been a seat of learning for more than 300 years.

Jack the Ripper?

On 10 October 1789, Joseph-Ignace Guillotin, a French physician, proposed that capital punishment should always take the form of decapitation "by means of a simple mechanism", as it was a less painful method of execution than had hitherto been employed. Thus the guillotine, indeed a simple mechanism for decapitation, became forever associated with the good doctor, despite the fact that he didn't invent it and was not himself in favour of the death penalty. Nevertheless, the guillotine became the favourite method for dispatching criminals and enemies of the state in France.

During the French Revolution, thousands were guillotined, mostly during the notorious Reign of Terror between 1793 and 1794. After the Revolution, the guillotine was retained as the preferred method of administering capital punishment. Following the abolition of the death penalty in France in 1981, the guillotine was finally retired from service. However, the final execution by guillotine took

The guillotine

place on 10 September 1977 in Marseille, when Hamida Djandoubi, who had earlier been convicted of the kidnap, torture and murder of his former girlfriend, was put to death. Djandoubi thus became the last person legally executed by beheading in the Western world, in the same year that the original *Star Wars* film was released. An unusual juxtaposition, I think you'll agree!

TWENTY-NINE

THE VEIL OF VERONICA

That a man named Jesus of Nazareth lived in Galilee around 2,000 years ago cannot be proven. Nevertheless, most historians today accept that he actually existed and was active during the period detailed in the New Testament. Whether you believe him to have been the Son of God, God the Son, a prophet, or just an ordinary human being will depend entirely on your own personal religious persuasion.

The death of Jesus by way of crucifixion and his subsequent resurrection are described in the Gospels of the New Testament. Again, whether you are inclined to believe this story to be factually accurate will depend upon your religious beliefs. Nevertheless, crucifixion as a means of capital punishment was common practice at that time in the Middle East.

According to legend, a woman named Veronica encountered Jesus in Jerusalem as he was carrying his cross to Calvary, his place of execution. She is said to have wiped the perspiration from his face with her veil, on to which the image of his face miraculously appeared. I use the term 'legend' because there is no mention of the story of Veronica in the Gospels, and the tale may simply be the result of mistranslation and elaboration. The Latin words '*vera*' and '*icon*' translate as 'truth' and 'image' respectively. Thus the 'Veil of Veronica' may actually mean the 'Veil of the True Image', and it has been argued that the veil might actually have been the cloth placed on the face of Jesus' body after he had been laid to rest. Either way, the Veil of Veronica is believed by many to be a true representation of the face of Jesus Christ.

Certainly, the image of a slender-faced man with long hair and a beard that we associate with Jesus today appears to stem from the image on the veil. The earliest recorded reference to the veil dates from only 1011 CE, and so, if genuine, begs the question of why there is no earlier record of the existence of such a miraculous relic. Nevertheless, early representations of the face of Jesus vary significantly, and it appears that it was only once the image on the veil had been popularised that the face of Jesus became stylised into the image we recognise today.

Early depictions of the face of Jesus

So, what does the image on the Veil of Veronica actually look like? Well, therein lies a problem. Following the Sack of Rome on 6 May 1527 by Charles V, contemporary sources claimed variously that the veil had either been destroyed, stolen or left entirely untouched. While the Vatican claimed to still be in possession of the veil, subsequent events cast doubt on this assertion. As a relic venerated by pilgrims, the veil was an important source of income for the papacy, and they would not have wanted to admit to it having been stolen or destroyed. Prior to 1527, many artists had made copies of the image and, interestingly, Pope Urban VIII ordered the destruction of all existing copies, leading many to suspect that they no longer had the original and had substituted a faked copy that would not stand up to scrutiny if compared to earlier first-hand copies of the genuine veil.

To this day, the Vatican claims that the Veil of Veronica that is held in St Peter's Basilica is the original veil, but the image appears to be little more than a dark, head-shaped blob, with no discerning features. Additionally, the image is displayed publicly only once a year, on Passion Sunday. On this occasion, the veil, in its heavy frame, is carried by three canons out on to the balcony above the statue of Saint Veronica. At this considerable distance, and with limited views, the image is barely observable. So, if the veil currently in the possession of the Vatican is a copy, did the original survive the Sack of Rome in 1527? Well, possibly.

Veil of Veronica, St Peter's Basilica

In 1999, Father Heinrich Pfeiffer claimed to have discovered the true Veil of Veronica, displayed in a church of the Capuchin monastery in the village of Manoppello, Italy. The image is much clearer than that of the Vatican's veil and depicts a face that we would recognise today as stylistically that of Jesus Christ. Apparently, the cloth is

The Manoppello Image

made from a rare fibre called 'byssus', which is occasionally found in the tombs of Egyptian pharaohs. Additionally, the image has not been painted on to the cloth. Professor Pfeiffer further claimed that he believed the veil to have been the cloth placed over Jesus' face in his tomb, and that the image was a by-product produced as a result of forces discharged from the body of Christ during the Resurrection. He further asserted that this was the same process that would explain the full body image of Jesus found on the more famous Shroud of Turin.

On 1 September 2006, Joseph Ratzinger, better known to all but his family and friends as Pope Benedict XVI, visited the Shrine

Pope Benedict XVI

of the Holy Face in Manoppello, knelt in veneration and prayed for several minutes before the image many believe to be the true Veil of Veronica. "Seeking the Face of Jesus must be the longing of all of us Christians," he said during his pilgrimage to the shrine. Thereafter, until his resignation, Pope Benedict XVI often made reference to "the human face of God in Christ". As Pope, he could never have actually stated that he believed the Manoppello Image to be the true Veil of Veronica. Nevertheless, his words and demeanour suggested that he considered it to be just that. Perhaps the Pope Emeritus knows something we don't!

THIRTY

HITLER'S SECOND BOOK

In 1958, during his summer holidays, an American scholar by the name of Gerhard Weinberg was trawling through German military documents captured by the USA at the end of World War II. His attention was drawn to a folder labelled 'Draft of Mein Kampf'. As he began to examine the yellowing 324-page typescript, it quickly became apparent to Weinberg that this was not, as stated, a draft of Hitler's famous 1925 publication.

References to an unpublished work by Adolf Hitler had been circulating, and a memoir by one of the Nazi leader's secretaries had made mention of a secret book about foreign policy. While of considerable interest to Weinberg, he had no idea where to even start looking for this elusive opus. Imagine his surprise and delight, therefore, when upon reading the opening lines of the pages before him he quickly realised that it must be the Fuhrer's missing tome. He later recalled his

Gerhard Weinberg in 2006

excitement at the discovery: "This thing in fact existed and was here! It really existed, it had survived. Lots of stuff, after all, had been destroyed."

In addition, the provenance was excellent. A brief report attached to the folder confirmed that it had been handed to an American officer in 1945 by Josef Berg, the manager of the Nazi publishing house, Eher Verlag, who said that it had been written at least 15 years previously. A witness also came forward to confirm that during the war Berg had shown him the manuscript of an unpublished book by Adolf Hitler. Additionally, it was apparent from erroneous spaces before commas and full stops that it had been dictated directly to a person using a typewriter, who had, on occasion, not correctly anticipated what was coming next. This was the method Hitler had employed to dictate *Mein Kampf*.

So, why was this second book not published during the lifetime of the Nazi leader? Apparently, it had been written during the summer of 1928,

Adolf Hitler (1889–1945)

around three years after the publication of *Mein Kampf*, which was not at that time selling well. Publication of a second book by the same author would have diluted sales of the first, and so it seems that the decision not to publish immediately after completion was a commercial one. The contents of the book may also have been a factor in the decision not to publish at a later date, after Hitler had risen to power.

Apparently, things did not pan out quite the way he had anticipated in 1928.

So, what did he say that prevented publication? Numerous things, it seems. Firstly, he attacked a number of right-wing politicians in the book, but later aligned himself with them for political purposes and so was unable to criticise them publicly before his ascent to power. This would not have been a problem after he became Chancellor, but by that time his foreign policy was somewhat different to the views expressed in his book.

The manuscript was never given a title and so was simply known as '*Zweites Buch*' (Second Book). In it, Hitler set out a plan, broken down into a number of stages. Firstly, he envisaged massive rearmament and the forging of alliances with both Italy and the UK. His rationale for an Anglo-German alliance was based on the notion that they were natural allies because the Anglo-Saxons, who had invaded and occupied Britain 1,500 years earlier, were of Germanic origin. The second stage involved a series of 'lightning wars', between Germany, Italy and Britain on the one side, and France and her allies in Eastern Europe on the other. The third stage necessitated the eradication of the communist regime in the Soviet Union.

While some of this could be gleaned from his 1925 publication, *Mein Kampf*, it was presumably deemed not in the best interests of either Hitler or the Nazi Party to publish new material proposing an alliance with the UK, especially once it had become apparent that not only was no such accord likely but that open hostility was a far more probable outcome.

In addition, in *Zweites Buch* he went a stage further. While accepting that in the short term the Soviet Union would be Germany's most dangerous opponent, Hitler stated that he regarded the USA as the most dangerous potential opponent in the longer term. While somewhat prophetic, it was not a view that Germany would likely have wanted to express publicly prior to the USA's actual entry into World War II in December 1941. He did, however, single out the USA as praiseworthy, owing to their practice of racial segregation and their adoption of eugenics to improve the genetic quality of the population.

From an academic perspective, Weinberg realised that it was important that the book should finally be published. And so it was that, in 1961, Hitler's *Zweites Buch* was published in German on a non-profit-making basis. A pirated version was also published in English, although, to quote Weinberg, the pirated translation was "lousy". More than 40 years later, an official English version, translated by Weinberg himself, was eventually published, in 2003.

So, what was it that drew the American scholar to this particular subject? Gerhard Weinberg was born in Hanover, Germany, in the same year as Hitler wrote his second book. The problem was that the Weinbergs were Jews, and so, as the Nazis rose to power, they had little choice but to leave their homeland. They travelled first to England in 1938, and then on to America, where they arrived in New York by passenger ship in 1940. Weinberg, who later adopted American citizenship, and his immediate family were the lucky ones. As many as six million Jews, including members of Weinberg's extended family, were murdered; victims of Hitler's 'final solution'.

THIRTY-ONE

MISADVENTURES IN TUDOR ENGLAND

The Darwin Awards, named in honour of the evolutionary theorist Charles Darwin, commemorate those who improve the human gene pool by removing themselves from it. That is to say, the recipient is someone who dies as a result of their own stupidity. Needless to say, the award is always given posthumously!

Take, for example, the case of an unnamed individual from Washington, DC, who decided to embark on a career of armed robbery in February 1990 by holding up a gun shop! Not only was the shop full of customers, but a uniformed police officer, whose patrol car was parked outside, was standing at the counter. The inept robber announced his arrival by informing those present of a hold-up and by firing some warning shots to show he meant business. To say he was out-gunned in the ensuing exchange of fire would be something of an understatement. The phrase 'more holes than a Swiss cheese' springs to mind.

Alternatively, there is the case of Mr Ken Barger of North Carolina, who thought it a good idea to keep a Smith & Wesson .38 Special next to his telephone on the bedside cabinet. I think you can see where this one is heading. On 21 December 1992, on being awoken by his ringing telephone, he reached for the receiver but unfortunately picked up the gun instead. He accidentally shot himself in the head.

As you might imagine, the ability to die in unfortunate circumstances is not a new phenomenon. History is littered with the corpses of those who died as a result of their own misfortune, or at the hands of other bungling individuals. Thanks to some excellent research, we have many examples of poor English Tudor folk who met their ends in untimely ways. What follows are some examples of fatal Tudor incompetence.

The condition of roads during the sixteenth century was appalling. Basically muddy tracks, they were heavily rutted by cartwheels and were either claggy in wet weather or rock hard when frozen or sun-baked. John Rusey was a labourer from Berkshire who preferred to wear his knife unsheathed and hanging loose from his belt. This proved to be his undoing because, on 11 March 1550, he was walking along a road in Chieveley when he tripped over 'carte rote' and fell forward. Yes, you've guessed it: he accidentally stabbed himself in the stomach. He was found dead by a neighbour on his way home from market.

When we think of hammer throwing today, we tend to imagine heavily muscled athletes launching projectiles towards a predetermined and unpopulated part of a sports field. Heavy-duty netting also features, in the event of wayward efforts. The Tudor equivalent would have given the gentleman of the Health and Safety Executive apoplexy! It seems that sledgehammers were launched with impunity whenever the will took. A number of cases were recorded of individuals being killed by flying hammers, but one of the most reckless must surely be that of Robert Woode, a weaver from Knowstone in Devon. On 2 July 1591, keen to demonstrate his prowess, he undertook an attempt to throw his hammer over a house. Unfortunately for Amicius Byckner, innocently passing by on the other side, he was successful.

Even piety had its pitfalls. On 22 November 1531, Mr Christopher Conyers, a gentleman of Brotton in Yorkshire, had spent the morning surveying his servants as they worked on his land. At about 11am, he sat down near the top of the coastal cliffs, got out his prayer book and began to commune with his maker. Having finished his supplication, he stood up and immediately lost his footing and slid over the edge of the cliff, falling about 150 feet to his death. A search party sent to look for him duly arrived at the cliff top and found only his reading glasses.

The relatively straightforward act of going to the toilet could also be deadly. An appropriately named baker from Cambridge, George Dunkyn, lived outside the equally appropriately named Trumpington Gate. On the evening of 2 June 1523, George needed to relieve himself. As he squatted over the cesspit in the corner of the garden, he lost his balance. He fell backwards off the board on which he had been perching and into the pit. According to the subsequent inquest, he was 'queasomed' to death. Apparently, he was very drunk at the time of the incident.

Preparing a solution of rat poison and then accidentally drinking it yourself is a fairly stupid way to die. But that is exactly what happened to Margaret Morlande of St Margaret, South Elmham in Suffolk. Before retiring for the night on 20 April 1599, she left a pot containing the deadly preparation standing beside a similar pot containing beer. Feeling thirsty in the night, she rose and reached out in the dark for the beer. What happened next needs no further explanation from me.

But perhaps the most poignant, and most tragic, example of mass ignorance occurred on Christmas Day 1502 at Colchester Castle. The dungeon of the castle, which was a confined space with walls 7 feet thick, contained 28 prisoners. They had managed to smuggle in firewood and planned to use it to facilitate a mass festive breakout. The plan was to set fire to the large wooden door and simply walk out once it had burned through. Sadly, the plan was doomed to failure because there was insufficient ventilation in the dungeon for such a large fire. Every single one of the prisoners was overcome by a combination of a lack of oxygen and the effects of smoke inhalation.

So, there you have it. As far as sheer stupidity goes, like everything else, we stand on the shoulders of giants!

THIRTY-TWO

THE REGICIDAL HERMIT

On Saturday, 30 January 1649, King Charles I was led
to the scaffold erected outside Banqueting House in
Whitehall, London. Apparently, it was a cold day, so the
King wore two thick shirts to ensure he didn't shiver
from the cold, so to avoid giving the impression of being
afraid. Charles asked the executioner to wait for him to
signal his readiness by outstretching his arms, to which
the executioner is reported to have replied: "Yes I will,
and it pleases your Majesty." Shortly thereafter the King
gave the sign and the executioner expertly severed his
head from his body in one blow. The crowd that had
gathered to witness the killing of a king reportedly
groaned in unison as the axe fell. Thus King Charles I
became the first, and so far only, British monarch to be
tried and executed. But what do we know of the man
who so deftly removed the head of the monarch?

What we do know is that no one seemed to want
the job. Richard Brandon, the London Hangman,

*King Charles I
(1600–1649)*

refused to carry out the deed despite being offered a significant sum of money. The identity of the actual executioner was certainly concealed – by false hair and beard, according to some accounts. When the body of Charles I was exhumed in 1813, it was confirmed that his head had indeed been smote from his body in a single strike, thus suggesting the work of a very competent axeman.

So, who did the deed? The simple answer is: we don't know. But one possible candidate was a man by the name of John Bigg. Bigg was clerk to Simon Mayne of Dinton in Buckinghamshire. Mayne was a judge and Member of Parliament for nearby Aylesbury, and one of the signatories on the death warrant of the King. After the Restoration of the Monarchy in 1660, he was tried, found guilty and sentenced to death. He died, however, while being held at the Tower of London in 1661, thus evading his own execution.

Bigg, being just an employee of Mayne, was not required to stand trial himself, and at just over 30 years of age, with a good education and being of not insignificant means, might have been expected to have simply looked for gainful employment elsewhere. What he did next, therefore, was surprising to say the least. He took up residence in a cave! Not only that, but he remained there for the rest of his life: some 35 years! He became completely reliant on the charity of locals for his sustenance, and also begged for scraps of leather. He sewed

*John Bigg
(1629–1696)*

or nailed the pieces of discarded leather to his clothes and shoes, the original material of the garments and footwear eventually being superseded entirely by the bits of old hide. If you happen to visit the Ashmolean Museum in Oxford, you can see one of his shoes on display there. A true curiosity if ever there was one!

So, what caused John Bigg to adopt this unconventional lifestyle? Certainly, it is possible that he had become mentally ill, perhaps due to the stress of being in the employ of a Parliamentarian at the time of the Restoration. However, he was not personally accused of any wrongdoing, so rumours began to circulate that perhaps Bigg had something more on his conscience than just a slightly dodgy CV. Was he the man who had donned a wig and false beard and separated the King's bean from his shoulders? No primary source documents have ever confirmed the identity of the executioner of King Charles I, so we will probably never know, but something certainly made Bigg seek the solitude of a cave for the rest of his life. Fear of retribution perhaps?

On the other hand, it seems unlikely that a clerk would have had the kind of axe-wielding ability capable of carrying out an execution with a single blow. Or was it just a case of beginner's luck?

Today, a pub near Aylesbury goes by the name of 'The Dinton Hermit'. Could it be that a more appropriate name for the hostelry should be 'The King's Head'?

THIRTY-THREE

ON TOP OF THE WORLD

At 29,029 feet, Mount Everest is the world's tallest mountain. By 1953, despite numerous attempts, no one had successfully scaled the Himalayan peak. That year, a British expedition led by John Hunt would attempt to become the first to conquer the summit. The team opted to try a route through the Khumbu Icefall and the South Col and, on 29 May, New Zealander, Edmund Hillary, and Nepalese Sherpa, Tenzing Norgay, using oxygen cylinders and masks, summited at 11.30am. Hillary buried a crucifix, while Norgay similarly interred sweets. Hillary took a photograph of Norgay standing on the summit, holding his ice axe strung with flags from the United Nations, India, Nepal and the UK. They spent about 15 minutes on the top of the world, before beginning their descent.

The success of the British expedition was announced on the eve of the coronation of Queen Elizabeth II and, as you might expect, there was much jubilation in the land!

The newly crowned Queen knighted Hillary on his return to Britain.

Sir Edmund Hillary and Sherpa Tenzing Norgay

However, while there is no doubt that Sir Edmund Hillary and Sherpa Tenzing Norgay were the first climbers to successfully climb Mount Everest, by reaching the top and coming back down again, were they really the first human beings to stand on the summit of the mountain? At the time of writing there is no definite answer to this question, but there remains a distinct possibility that they were not. British climbers, George Mallory and Andrew 'Sandy' Irvine, were part of an expedition that set out to climb the mountain in 1924, almost 30 years before Hillary and Norgay's ascent. On 8 June 1924, armed with a camera and a rudimentary oxygen supply, the pair left high camp to make an attempt at the summit, and were seen by fellow climber, Noel Odell, on the north-east ridge of Everest, just a few hundred yards from the summit.

The following is an excerpt from Odell's account: "At 12.50… there was a sudden clearing of the atmosphere, and the entire summit ridge and final peak of Everest were unveiled. My eyes became fixed on one tiny black spot silhouetted on a small snow crest beneath a rock step in the ridge; the black spot moved. Another black spot became apparent and moved up the snow to join the other on the crest. The first then approached the great rock step and shortly emerged at the top; the second did likewise. Then the whole fascinating vision vanished, enveloped in cloud once more."

Sadly, Odell's sighting was the last time either man was seen alive. That they both died on Everest is a certainty. What is unknown is whether they were ascending or descending the mountain at the time of their deaths and, if descending, had they reached the summit or had they been forced to turn back before reaching the top? For many years, the only evidence to go on was Odell's account, suggesting that they were closing in on the summit when last seen.

However, on 1 May 1999, the body of George Mallory, wearing a tweed suit, was discovered at the bottom of a snowfield on the North Face, at 26,760 feet. His mummified body was sun-bleached and frozen, and he had suffered fractures to his right leg. The fatal injury, however, was a large puncture wound to his forehead. A rope tied around his waist led to a broken end, suggesting he and Irvine were together when they suffered an accident.

But, interestingly, it was the contents of his pockets that yielded further tantalising clues. Mallory was known to be carrying a photograph of his wife, Ruth, which he had planned to leave on the summit. There

George Mallory

was no photograph on his body, leading many to believe that they had summited and he had left the photograph on the top of Everest as intended. Secondly, his snow goggles were in his pocket, suggesting that he was descending in fading light when the accident occurred. Given the time of day the pair were spotted by Odell, they would have had more than sufficient time to have reached the summit and begun descending before the onset of twilight. Unfortunately, Mallory was not carrying the camera, nor was it found near to his body. George Mallory's remains were covered with a cairn on the spot where he had come to rest 75 years earlier.

Expert mountaineer and conqueror of Everest, Chris Bonington, offered the following assessment:

> If we accept the fact that they were above the Second Step, they would have seemed to be incredibly close to the summit of Everest, and I think at that stage something takes hold of most climbers... And I think therefore, taking all those circumstances in view... I think it is quite conceivable that they did go for the summit... I certainly would love to think that they actually reached the summit of Everest. I think it is a lovely thought and I think it is something, you know, gut emotion, yes I would love them to have got there. Whether they did or not, I think that is something one just cannot know.

Despite a number of searches, the body of Irvine has not been found. Experts from Kodak believe that, if the camera could be found, it should be possible, with extreme care, to develop any images contained on the film inside. Somewhere below that icy peak lies the body of Andrew Irvine, and a camera. If only that camera could be located, what a story it could tell!

Andrew 'Sandy' Irvine

THIRTY-FOUR

THE MYSTERY OF CHRISTIE

Agatha Miller was born on 15 September 1890, the third child of American stockbroker, Frederick Miller, and his wife, Clara. A wealthy family, they lived in a villa named Ashfield in the coastal town of Torquay in the English county of Devon. Although the family home was in the south-west of the country, Agatha also spent a good deal of time with her aunt and step-grandmother at their home in Ealing, west London. The early years that she spent in the metropolis would bear much ripe fruit later in her life. Agatha always described her childhood as "very happy". However, in November 1901, her father, who had been in poor health for some time, died, aged only 55. Although just 11 years old at the time, Agatha claimed that her father's death marked the end of her childhood.

In about 1913, Agatha met Archibald Christie at a dance held near to her home in Torquay. Archie, as he was known, was an army officer who had become a member of the fledgling Royal Flying Corps. With World War I looming on the horizon, Archie and Agatha decided to get married as soon as possible. That date turned out to be Christmas Eve 1914, while Archie was home on leave.

Young Agatha

In the decades to come, her married name of Agatha Christie would become synonymous with the murder mystery genre of writing. After the war, the couple took a flat in St John's Wood, London.

Agatha Christie's first novel was published in 1919, and in that same year she gave birth to her only child, a daughter named Rosalind Margaret. As her literary career began to take off, and with Archie now gainfully employed in the financial sector, all seemed rosy in the Christie household. They travelled widely, visiting such far-flung destinations as Hawaii, South Africa and Australia, and were quite possibly the first English man and woman to learn how to surf standing upright. Agatha later wrote in her autobiography: "I learned to become expert, or at any rate expert from a European point of view – the moment of complete triumph on the day I kept my balance and came right onto shore standing upright on my board." In short, family life for the Christies seemed idyllic. Then, to the complete surprise of her burgeoning fan base, Agatha Christie disappeared!

Archibald Christie

Agatha's disappearance made headlines on both sides of the Atlantic

On 3 December 1926, her secretary discovered a note from Christie in which she said she was going to Yorkshire. Her car was later found parked above a chalk quarry, near Guildford in Surrey. In it were her driving licence and clothes. A massive hunt ensued, with around 1,000 police officers and 15,000 volunteers involved in the search. Aircraft were even deployed in pursuit of the missing author. Agatha Christie was eventually discovered on 14 December, staying at the Swan Hydropathic Hotel in Harrogate, Yorkshire, under the name Mrs Neele. So, what had caused the successful novelist to stage her own disappearance? As you can probably guess, all was not quite what it seemed. Agatha's mother had passed away earlier in the year, and her grief was compounded when her husband confessed to infidelity, having fallen in love with another woman. Archie had asked for a divorce shortly before her dramatic vanishing act. Although Agatha herself never offered an explanation for her erratic behaviour, the most poignant clue was the alias of Mrs Neele that she gave to the hotel receptionist upon checking in. The name of Archie's mistress was Nancy Neele!

Public reaction was not positive, with many suggesting a publicity stunt, or even an attempt to frame Archie and Nancy for murder. A more likely explanation is that she was simply in a fragile mental state and needed to get away from it all for a while.

Agatha and Archie were divorced in 1928 and Archie soon married Nancy. Agatha was given custody of their daughter and also retained the name of Christie for professional purposes because this was the name by which she was known to her readers worldwide. Agatha herself remarried in 1930. Her second husband was Max Mallowan, an eminent archaeologist, and they remained happily married for almost 46 years.

Max and Agatha

Agatha Christie's two most acclaimed fictional characters were Hercule Poirot, a Belgian detective based in London, and Miss Jane Marple, an elderly amateur sleuth who lived in the equally fictional village of St Mary Mead. Following the publication of her novel, *Curtain,* in which Poirot dies, he became the only fictional character to receive an obituary in *The New York Times!* Agatha always maintained that the character of Jane Marple was based on an amalgamation of her step-grandmother and her "Ealing cronies". She remarked that both gran and the fictional Jane "always expected the worst of everyone and everything, and were, with almost frightening accuracy, usually proved right."

Another mysterious episode, or rather coincidence, involving Agatha occurred during World War II. In her novel, *N or M?,* a character named Major Bletchley claims to have knowledge of crucial British wartime secrets. At the time, Christie was friends with Dilly Knox, a cryptographer working at Bletchley Park in Buckinghamshire, Britain's top-secret codebreaking establishment. MI5 were alarmed and wondered whether Knox had passed information to Christie because she seemed to be aware of the name of an

Bletchley Park, home of the codebreakers

institute that was not supposed to exist. Knox was adamant that he hadn't told her anything and approached Agatha to establish the origin of the name of the character. It transpired that it was the result of a delayed train. She told Knox: "Bletchley? My dear, I was stuck there on my way by train from Oxford to London and took revenge by giving the name to one of my least loveable characters."

Agatha passed away on 12 January 1976 at the age of 85. She was laid to rest in the churchyard of St Mary's, Cholsey, in south Oxfordshire, close to the house where she had lived with Max. She was survived by both her husband and her daughter Rosalind.

THIRTY-FIVE

THE WORLD'S
WEIRDEST WARS

War is not normally an amusing subject. Most
commonly, wars occur as a result of disputes over
territory or religion, with death and injury the inevitable
consequences. In what follows, I do not intend to make
light of the seriousness of the subject, but there are
occasions in history where wars broke out for the oddest
of reasons or were fought in the strangest of ways. Below
are examples of some of the world's weirdest wars.

Where to begin? Well, let's go back in time to
1325 and have a look at the **War of the Bucket.** Yes,
that's right, a war began over a bucket! Two city states,
Bologna and Modena, in modern-day Italy, were not
exactly ideal neighbours: one came under the control
of the Holy Roman Empire, while the other remained
loyal to the papacy. Nevertheless, peace reigned. Until,
that is, a few soldiers from Modena popped over to
Bologna and pinched a bucket from a well.

Bologna immediately declared war on Modena. At 32,000 strong, the army raised by Bologna heavily outnumbered the 7,000 men put up by the shocked Modenese. The armies met in November 1325 at Zappolino, in Bolognese territory. Despite their numerical advantage, and regardless of the fact that they were on home soil, the Bolognese were heavily defeated and forced to flee the battlefield. In all, about 4,000 men died in a conflict ostensibly fought over a bucket!

So, what became of the bucket? Well, it remains on display to this day in the city of Modena. Surely beyond the 'pail'. Sorry!

Moving forward in time, to 1859 in fact, to the San Juan Islands on the Canadian/American border, we are just in time for the **Pig War**. The British, always keen to claim new territory, had set up a colony on the islands to farm sheep, but the Americans, deciding the land was theirs, sent 25 of their own people to settle there. For a time, the British and American settlers seemed to rub along together in relative harmony.

However, on 15 June 1859, an American by the name of Lyman Cutlar spotted a pig rifling through his vegetable patch. Not one to take such things lightly, Cutlar exercised his right to bear arms, and shot the pig dead, mid potato. Unfortunately for Anglo-American relations, the owner of the pig was one Charles Griffin, an Irishman residing on the British side of the islands. Needless to say, Griffin was singularly unimpressed that his pig had been cut down in its prime. He rejected Cutlar's offer of 10 dollars by way of compensation, instead demanding 100 dollars for the slain animal.

Things escalated alarmingly from thereon in. The British tried to arrest Cutlar, who by this time had requested assistance from the USA. The Americans, for some reason, felt it necessary to send 66 soldiers to his defence. The British took umbrage at this and deployed two warships to the islands. By 10 August, things had got even worse. There were now five warships and over 2,000 men on the scene for the British. The Americans had around 460 soldiers with 14 cannons, presumably all pointing towards the British vessels.

The result of all this was something of a Mexican standoff, although it took a full 12 years before tensions finally subsided. In the end, the only casualty of the Pig War was the hapless pig, although the cost to both sides must have exceeded even Griffin's exaggerated valuation by a factor of thousands!

During the early part of the twentieth century, Greece and Bulgaria were like a couple of neighbours arguing over where to put the fence. The border region of Petrich was hotly disputed, although, prior to 22 October 1925, an uneasy peace endured. On that fateful day, however, an unnamed Greek soldier was seen chasing a dog. The dog crossed the border into Bulgaria, and the unwitting soldier followed it. The Bulgarian guard on duty at the time did not mess about. He shot and killed the soldier.

The following day, Greece invaded Petrich in response.

The Pig War

The Bulgarians were unprepared, and the Greeks made significant inroads. After 10 days of fighting, the League of Nations intervened and demanded an immediate ceasefire. In total, around 100 people lost their lives in the **War of the Stray Dog.** The fate of the dog remains unknown.

Following the collapse of the Soviet Union, the country of Moldova was in crisis. The majority of the population wanted a closer association with Romania, while the remainder preferred an alliance with Russia. The result was that, in 1992, the **Moldovan–Transnistrian War** broke out. Nothing particularly weird about that, I agree. What makes this war unusual is the way in which it was fought.

By day, soldiers of the opposing armies fought each other in traditional fashion, each trying to kill the other. By night, however, the fighting would stop, and the protagonists would meet up for a drink! It turned out that they actually got along like a house on fire. So well, in fact, that they decided to stop trying to shoot each other during the day. After four months of ever-diminishing animosity, peace broke out. It is unfortunate that both sides suffered several hundred casualties before the thing basically petered out of its own accord. Technically, hostilities concluded with a ceasefire, but most combatants had ceased firing well before it officially ended.

In 1883, King Alfonso XII of Spain was on an official state visit to Paris. For some reason best known to the French, a few Parisians elected to hurl insults at the monarch, and a number even tried to assault him. As a result of this heinous insult, the mayor of Lijar, a small town in southern Spain, became almost apoplectic. He immediately declared war on France, and most of the 300 residents of the town were apparently right behind him. So began the **Lijar–French War.**

In 1977, King Juan Carlos of Spain, no doubt aware of his predecessor's Gallic welcome, nevertheless chanced his arm, and visited France himself. To his undoubted relief, nothing untoward occurred, and his visit passed off peacefully. In 1981, the good people of Lijar met and decided that, owing to the dignified manner in which their reigning monarch had been treated by the French, they would end hostilities forthwith. In the 98 years of conflict not a single shot was fired, and there were no casualties. Now, that's my kind of war!

King Alfonso XII of Spain

THIRTY-SIX

JOHN HAMPDEN: FATHER OF DEMOCRACY?

Prior to the English Civil War (1642–1651), the power of the reigning monarch was absolute. They ruled by divine right, meaning their authority came from God, and no subject was at liberty to question that authority, let alone take up arms against their sovereign. The eventual outcome of the war was the establishment of the constitutional precedent that the monarch required the consent of Parliament in order to have authority to govern. The rule by divine right was at an end, and the seeds of democratic government had been sown. Today, modern democracies the world over can trace their roots back to this tumultuous period of English history.

The credit for this monumental overhaul of government is generally afforded to Oliver Cromwell (1599–1658), who was one of the principal commanders of the Parliamentarian army and a signatory to the death warrant of King Charles I in 1649 (for more detail on the execution, see my earlier story entitled 'The Regicidal Hermit?'). From 1653 until his death, Cromwell was known as 'Lord Protector of the Commonwealth', a grand title for a democrat! However, there is also a man who, were it not for his untimely death, might also be known today as one of the fathers of democracy. That man was John Hampden (c.1595–1643), a rather overlooked character these days given his importance at the time.

Oliver Cromwell (1599–1658)

John Hampden was born in 1594 or 1595 in London to a wealthy family with landholdings in both Buckinghamshire and Middlesex. He was educated at Thame School in Oxfordshire, and Magdalen College, Oxford. As the eldest son, he inherited his family's estates on the death of his father and, in addition, sat as the Member of Parliament for Wendover in Buckinghamshire during the reign of King Charles I.

Charles was an unpopular king, suspected of having Catholic sympathies, and continually obliging his wealthier subjects to offer him loans or pay higher taxes in order to raise funds for wars abroad that the country could ill afford. Having already been imprisoned in 1627 for refusing to pay a forced loan to the King, the tipping point for Hampden came in 1637, when the King came up with a new wheeze to raise funds by extending the scope of a tax known as 'ship money'.

John Hampden (c.1595–1643)

King Charles I
(1600–1649)

Basically, ship money was a tax paid by coastal counties for naval defence. Charles argued that all counties should pay ship money because the defence of the coast was ultimately in the interest of all counties, not just those with a coastline. In this he was quite right. A modern analogy would be that of a block of flats, where everyone is obliged to contribute to the maintenance of the roof, not just those living in the top flats. However, it was immediately apparent that the King was not merely trying to share the tax burden more equitably, as his argument suggested, but actually attempting to increase it. His plan was to charge each individual county the same amount as he had previously charged individual coastal counties only, thus almost doubling the revenue from this method of taxation.

Accepting the validity of the King's argument, Hampden did not refuse to pay ship money but refused to pay the full amount, thereby highlighting the inequity of Charles's position. Needless to say, the King was not pleased. Nevertheless, matters proceeded disagreeably but peacefully enough, until the King's patience snapped, on 4 January 1642, when he entered the English House of Commons accompanied by armed soldiers, intent on arresting John Hampden and four other Members of Parliament on charges of treason. Presumably having been forewarned, the individuals in question were not present when the King entered the chamber, so the attempt was unsuccessful.

However, the incident demonstrated that the King was prepared to use force against Parliament, and this proved to be the catalyst for the ensuing Civil War.

Upon the outbreak of hostilities, Hampden raised a regiment of foot soldiers from his Buckinghamshire estates. The Greencoat Regiment, as they were known, fought with distinction, eventually forcing the King and his army to retreat to Oxford. The university city thus became a stronghold for Royalist forces, with their Parliamentarian opponents positioning themselves at the market town of Thame, a few miles away. And so it was that the two places with which Hampden was so familiar from his student days became bitterly opposed to one another.

Sadly, however, John Hampden would not live to see the birth of democracy. On 18 June 1643, at the Battle of Chalgrove Field, he was attempting to discharge a pistol, which instead of firing exploded in his hand, causing serious injuries and necessitating his withdrawal. He returned to his headquarters at the Greyhound Inn in Thame, now a shoe shop, where he died of his injuries on 24 June 1643. The pistol was one of a pair given to him by his son-in-law, Sir Robert Pye, and Hampden was initially of the opinion that Pye was responsible for his accident by having provided him with sub-standard weaponry. However, when Pye examined the other pistol, it transpired that it was loaded with numerous charges. It seemed that a servant, tasked with loading the pistols every morning, had done so meticulously but without removing the previous day's charge first!

For reasons that are not entirely clear, the English have a strange habit of digging up their heroes and

*Statue of John
Hampden in
Aylesbury,
Buckinghamshire*

villains after a couple of hundred years or so. Hampden was no exception. An exhumation took place in 1828, which revealed extensive damage to the bones of his right hand. This effectively confirmed the contemporary account of the exploding pistol and laid to rest a rumour that he had actually been shot in the shoulder by a Royalist marksman.

To this day, the independence of the House of Commons is ceremonially epitomised every year at the State Opening of Parliament. Traditionally, the door of the Commons is slammed in the face of a senior officer of the House of Lords known as 'Black Rod', to symbolise its independence from the monarchy. Would John Hampden have approved of this discourteous demonstration of parliamentary defiance? Absolutely!

THIRTY-SEVEN

REST IN PEACE?

Following on from my previous story about John Hampden, the English politician and nemesis of King Charles I, during which I mentioned the peculiar English habit of digging up the corpses of important people long after they've been laid to rest, I decided to look a little deeper into this strange compulsion.

Unsurprisingly, it seems, dead monarchs are no exception. Indeed, the chances of a deceased sovereign resting in peace in perpetuity does not seem to be terribly high. Excluding King Richard III, whose remains, you may recall, were discovered beneath a car park in Leicester, England, in 2012 during an archaeological dig, the mortal remains of at least 10 other crowned heads have been exhumed over the years. What follows is a brief summary of those disinterments.

Edward the Confessor (1003–1066) died on 5 January 1066 and was buried in Westminster Abbey, which was still under construction at the time. For some reason, Henry I ordered his tomb to be opened in 1102. It was reported that the corpse had not decayed, and this was taken to be a sign of the late King's saintliness. He was eventually canonised by Pope Alexander III in 1161. Saint Edward, as he was then known, had his eternal rest interrupted again in 1163, this time at the behest of Henry II. The body was found to have been wrapped in a cloth of gold, which Henry quickly appropriated, replacing it with a silk cloth. The gold cloth was subsequently made into "three splendid copes" (capes). The poor old saint, or jack-in-the-box, was disturbed again in 1685, when workmen dropped a rafter, which fell into the coffin. A gold chain and an enamelled crucifix were discovered and given to King James II. These succeeding monarchs seem to have been little better than grave robbers!

King John (1166–1216) died on 18 October 1216 and was buried at Worcester Cathedral. His repose lasted until 1797 when, purportedly in the interests of academic research, his tomb was opened. The remains of a sword and scabbard lay at his side, and his mortal remains were covered by a robe, the embroidery of which had deteriorated. He was just over 5 feet 6 inches tall. Fascinating stuff, I presume, if you're an academic!

King John

Edward I (1239–1307) was also known as 'Edward Longshanks', owing to the fact that he was a tall man for his time. He died on 7 July 1307 and was interred at Westminster Abbey. His tomb was opened in 1774 by the Society of Antiquaries, presumably out of academic interest. He was richly dressed and had been wrapped in linen cloth. In his right hand was a sceptre, and in his left hand a rod around 5 feet long and a white enamel dove. He was 6 feet 2 inches tall. Reasonably lofty, even by today's standards.

Richard II (1367–1400) died in captivity in Pontefract Castle in February 1400, having been deposed by his successor, Henry IV. He was initially laid to rest in Kings Langley Church in Hertfordshire, before being

Edward I

moved in 1413 to Westminster Abbey, where he was re-interred next to his wife, Anne. During restoration work in 1871, their tomb was opened. Well, of course it was! The only thing to do when undertaking a bit of restoration work! In addition to the two skeletons, the tomb contained a staff, sceptre, gloves and the remains of shoes. It also appears that a number of relics were taken from the tomb at this time. A cigarette box, annotated '31 August 1871, Westminster Abbey', was found recently in the basement of the National Portrait Gallery in London and contained fragments of wood, fabric and leather.

This next one takes exhumation to a whole other level. Catherine of Valois (1401–1437) was the wife of Henry V and died in childbirth on 3 January 1437. She was buried at Westminster Abbey, where she remained undisturbed until 1667 when she was exhibited to visitors by Abbey staff in return for the payment of a fee! The diarist Samuel Pepys recorded that, on a visit, he was permitted to embrace the remains. Even worse, he noted: "I had the upper part of her body in my hands, and I did kiss her mouth, reflecting upon it that I did kiss a queen." Yes, he actually kissed a 230-year-old corpse on the mouth. It's enough to put you off your dinner!

Edward IV (1442–1483) died on 9 April 1483 and was buried in St George's Chapel, Windsor Castle. During restoration work in 1789, his tomb was rediscovered and opened. Naturally! The lead coffin contained his skeleton, some long brown hair, and a dark liquid, presumed to be the result of bodily decomposition. Relics were taken, including locks of hair and a phial of the putrid liquid. Lovely!

Edward V (1470–c.1483) reigned for just 86 days – from the death of his father, Edward IV, until succeeded by his uncle, Richard III. Edward and his younger brother Richard disappeared after being held at the Tower of London. Responsibility for their disappearance was attributed to Richard III, although this has never been proven. In 1674, during work at the Tower, a wooden box was unearthed that contained the skeletal remains of two children. They were eventually re-interred at Westminster Abbey. An examination of the bones in 1933 concluded that they were of the correct ages for the missing brothers. With the discovery of the remains of Richard III in 2012, a sample of DNA from the bones should be all that is required to settle the matter of the identity of the children once and for all. However, both the Church of England and Queen Elizabeth II have refused to allow forensic testing of the remains, on the basis that it could set a precedent that would lead to multiple royal disinterments. Honestly, the one time that an exhumation would serve a useful purpose, and they veto it!

Anne Boleyn (1501–1536), second wife of Henry VIII, was executed at the Tower of London on 19 May 1536, having been found guilty of adultery, incest and high treason, despite the evidence against her being highly questionable. She was interred in an unmarked grave in the Chapel of St Peter and Vincula, being the parish church in the vicinity of the Tower. Over the ensuing years, the chapel's pavement began to subside, and in 1876 it was decided to replace it. When the original pavement was lifted, the bones of a female were discovered. A surgeon who examined the remains concluded that they were of a woman of about 5 feet 3 inches in height and of a delicate frame of body.

Anne Boleyn

Edward VI (1537–1553) died, probably of tuberculosis, on 6 July 1553 and was buried in the Henry VII Lady Chapel at Westminster Abbey. During a survey of the royal burial vaults in 1871, a coffin in poor condition was discovered. A plate on the lid confirmed the remains to be those of Edward VI. Without disturbing the contents, it was noted that the skeleton and remnants of a skullcap were visible.

Charles I (1600–1649) was beheaded on 30 January 1649, and his remains were laid to rest in St George's Chapel, Windsor Castle. For reasons not entirely clear, his coffin was opened in 1813, and his severed head was found to be in remarkable condition. The skin was discoloured, but his beard was in a perfect state of preservation and many teeth remained in place. The head was, unsurprisingly,

*Edward VI
(1537–1553)*

*King Charles I
(1600–1649)*

found to be loose, and so it was removed and examined. The back of his scalp was in such a good state of preservation that even the pores of the skin were discernible. His hair was dark brown. It also appeared that the executioner had done an excellent job; the fourth cervical vertebra had been sliced through perfectly!

THIRTY-EIGHT

THE DISAPPEARANCE OF CORA CRIPPEN

Hawley Harvey Crippen was a small, mild-mannered man. At just 5 feet 4 inches in height, of slight build and bespectacled, perhaps the only noticeable feature of this otherwise unremarkable man was his large walrus moustache. His wife, on the other hand, was an extremely noticeable individual. Cora Crippen was an unsuccessful music hall singer who liked to have a good time. Of stout build, a heavy drinker and promiscuous, Cora dominated her husband, and humiliated him with a string of adulterous relationships. Cuckolded and browbeaten, the lot of Hawley Harvey Crippen was not a happy one!

Dr Crippen, as he preferred to be known, was born in Coldwater, Michigan, USA, in 1862. He obtained qualifications in homeopathic medicine and began a practice in New York City, where he met and married his second wife, Cora, in 1894.

Cora Crippen

In 1897, the couple moved to London, England, despite the fact that Crippen's qualifications were insufficient to permit him to practise as a medical doctor in the UK. Nevertheless, he continued to use the prefix 'Dr' while actually working as a dispenser of medicines. In 1899, he became the manager of an institution for the treatment of the deaf, where, in about 1903, he met a young typist by the name of Ethel Le Neve – but more of her shortly.

Despite the move to England, Cora's music hall career, under the stage name of Belle Elmore, remained in the doldrums, and so it was on Dr Crippen's modest income that the couple were mostly reliant. In 1905, the husband and wife took up residence at 39 Hilldrop Crescent, Camden Road, in the London suburb of Holloway, where, in order to supplement Crippen's meagre earnings, they took in lodgers. It was upon returning home one day that Crippen discovered his wife in flagrante with one of them.

Hawley Harvey Crippen

Mild mannered he may have been, but this latest act of adultery caused Crippen to look elsewhere for solace, and so it was that, in about 1908, he began a relationship with Ethel, the typist he had met some five years earlier. The dysfunctional marriage stumbled on for a couple more years, until things came to a head following a party at 39 Hilldrop Crescent on 31 January 1910. The following day, Dr Crippen announced that his wife had decided to return to the USA for an extended holiday, later adding that she had sadly passed away while there and had been cremated in California.

In the meantime, Crippen had moved Ethel into Hilldrop Crescent, and she was even seen wearing clothing and jewellery belonging to Cora. Friends of Cora grew suspicious and asked the police to investigate. The house was duly searched, and Crippen was interviewed by Chief Inspector Walter Dew of Scotland Yard. Nothing untoward was uncovered by the search, and Crippen admitted to Dew that he had made up the story about Cora being dead, claiming that she had actually left him and gone to America with a lover. His fabrication, he maintained, was due to the shame he felt at his wife's immoral behaviour.

The chief inspector was quite happy with Crippen's explanation and planned to take no further action in the case. However, the intervention of the police appears to have panicked Crippen because the following day both he and Ethel took flight. They travelled firstly to Belgium, from where they boarded an ocean liner called the SS *Montrose*, bound for Canada. Naturally, Dew's suspicions were raised by Crippen's sudden disappearance, and as a result he decided to carry out a more detailed search at Hilldrop Crescent. Upon lifting the brick floor of the basement, the pungent odour of rotting flesh immediately filled the room, and the police uncovered a human torso, minus head, limbs and sexual organs. The torso was identified by a pathologist as belonging to Cora Crippen, due to the presence of a scar that corresponded with an operation she had undergone.

Unsurprisingly, the murder investigation, as it now was, became a media sensation, and the hunt to track down Crippen and Ethel was on. Meanwhile, Henry George Kendall, Captain of the SS *Montrose*, had had his attention drawn to the unusual behaviour of two of his passengers. A Mr Robinson, travelling with his teenage son, was seen to be acting in an overly affectionate manner towards the boy, giving the pair the appearance of a courting couple. Alerted to the hunt for the fugitives, Kendall immediately saw through their flimsy disguise. As the ship was still just within wireless range of the UK, he alerted the British authorities of their presence on his ship by way of a telegram.

Chief Inspector Dew wasted no time and quickly boarded the SS *Laurentic*, a faster liner than the *Montrose*, sailing from Liverpool, England, to Quebec, Canada. The story was now headline news around the world. With sexual impropriety, a gruesome murder, lovers fleeing in disguise and a race across the Atlantic, this one seemingly had it all! Newspapers carried daily updates on the progress of the *Laurentic* against the *Montrose*. Crippen and Ethel had become infamous overnight, and they were just about the only ones who didn't know it!

To the undoubted relief of the chief inspector, the *Laurentic* arrived in Quebec ahead of the *Montrose*, and Dew quickly notified the Canadian authorities of his intention to apprehend the wanted duo. As soon as the *Montrose* entered the St Lawrence River, the British bobby boarded the ship, disguised as a river pilot. Dr Crippen and Ethel Le Neve were arrested on 31 July 1910 and brought back to England to face trial for the murder of Cora Crippen. The case thus became the first time that fugitives had been apprehended by use of the wireless telegraph.

Throughout his trial, Crippen maintained that his wife had merely left him and gone to live in the USA with her lover. He further contended that, as they had only lived at 39 Hilldrop Crescent since 1905, the remains discovered must have been placed under the cellar floor by a previous occupant. He showed little emotion during the proceedings and expressed concern only for the reputation of Ethel. The jury were not convinced by his story and took just 27 minutes to find him guilty of murder. Hawley Harvey Crippen was executed at Pentonville Prison, London, at 9am on 23 November 1910. He was 48 years old. The charge against Ethel Le Neve was merely that of being an accessory after the fact, and she was duly acquitted. In accordance with his wishes, a photograph of Ethel was buried with him.

Dr Crippen and Ethel Le Neve at a remand hearing

Intriguingly, however, that is not the end of this sad story. For those who like a twist in the tale, this one finishes up in a positive knot! In October 2007, it was announced that a sample of DNA extracted from the scar tissue that had been used to identify the torso in 1910 had been repeatedly tested against samples obtained from grand-nieces of Cora Crippen. Not only did they not match, but the presence of a Y chromosome in the sample from the deceased indicated that the remains were not even that of a woman! So, if the body in the basement was not that of Cora, who was the mutilated victim? And what of Cora? Did Dr Crippen really murder his wife? If so, what did he do with her? Or is it possible that he was telling the truth after all? Oh dear!

THIRTY-NINE

JOHN STRINGFELLOW: THE FATHER OF POWERED FLIGHT

If you ask the question, "Who was the first person to achieve powered flight using a heavier-than-air aircraft?", the answer most people will give you is Orville Wright. Some, particularly those who read my earlier story entitled 'Wright? Wrong!', will gleefully tell you that it was actually Gustave Whitehead. Certainly, Gustave, who took to the air in August 1901, seems to have beaten the Wright brothers – who didn't get off the ground until December 1903 – to it by more than two years. Either way, the momentous achievement of both Whitehead and the Wrights was that they actually flew in a heavier-than-air aircraft. But in order to correctly answer the above question, we will need to go all the way back to 1848, to the town of Chard in Somerset, England.

John Stringfellow was born in Sheffield, England, in 1799 and earned his living in Chard as a maker of bobbins and carriages for the lacemaking industry. However, in collaboration with an inventor by the name of William Samuel Henson, the pair were awarded British patent 9478 in 1842 for an aerial steam carriage, known simply as the 'Aerial'.

An artist's impression of the Aerial

The design was for a monoplane with a wingspan of 150 feet, to be powered by a steam engine producing 50 horsepower. Stringfellow and Henson anticipated carrying 10 to 12 passengers at a top speed of 50 miles per hour for up to 1,000 miles. The undercarriage was a three-wheeled design, and the intention was that it would take off from an inclined ramp. However, owing to the poor power-to-weight ratio of the hefty steam engine, the design was simply too heavy and underpowered to be capable of flying and, consequently, a full-scale version of the Aerial was never constructed.

Instead, Henson and Stringfellow produced a progression of scale models of the design, initially without much success. A model built by Henson in 1843 managed only a tentative hop, as the inventor continued to grapple with the difficulty of using steam-powered technology in an aircraft. He subsequently built a larger model with a 20-foot wingspan but, despite numerous attempts between 1844 and 1847, it too failed to fly. Shortly thereafter, Henson emigrated to the USA, settling in Newark, New Jersey; and, while continuing to work on new inventions, he undertook little more in the way of aviation research.

John Stringfellow

William Samuel Henson

Stringfellow, meanwhile, had been working on his own model: a monoplane with a 10-foot wingspan, powered by a tiny 3-kilogram steam engine which he had also built. The machine had a wooden frame covered in silk, and the engine, housed in a gondola beneath the wings, powered two large propellers.

In early 1848, Stringfellow's contraption was ready for testing. All he needed now was a safe environment in which to make the first attempt at powered flight. Fortunately, he was able to secure the loan of a long room in a disused lace factory in Chard. The room was approximately 20 metres long and almost 4 metres in height. The model was to be launched from an inclined wire, so as to give it sufficient altitude to be able to continue airborne once operating under its own steam.

However, the first attempt almost ended in disaster. The adjustable tail had been set at too steep an angle, and the machine stalled and fell backwards, landing on, and breaking, the tail. Undeterred, Stringfellow repaired the tail, set it at a less acute angle and prepared to go again. What happened next is probably best left to Stringfellow's son, Fred, to describe: "The steam was again got up, and the machine started down the wire, and, upon reaching the point of self-detachment, it gradually rose until it reached the farther end of the room, striking a hole in the canvas placed to stop it. In experiments the machine flew well, when rising as much as one in seven."

So, there you have it. On an undetermined date in 1848, although thought to have been sometime in June, it was in a disused lace mill in Chard, Somerset, England that, for the first time in history, a heavier-than-air aircraft actually lifted into the air.

Stringfellow was subsequently invited to bring his flying machine to London, where, at Crenmore Gardens, demonstrations of the machine's ability were witnessed by many. The longest flight achieved by the machine was approximately 37 metres, although it would have gone further but for the canvas sheeting strategically placed to stop it.

Stringfellow's flying machine

John Stringfellow's flying machine can be viewed today at London's Science Museum, and a bronze model of the world's first powered aircraft stands proudly in Fore Street, Chard. Shortly before he died in 1883, Stringfellow made the following self-deprecating comment: "Somebody must do better than I before we succeed with aerial navigation."

Given the technology at his disposal, John Stringfellow almost certainly took powered flight about as far as it was possible to go during the first half of the nineteenth century. With the invention of the internal combustion engine, and its vastly superior power-to-weight ratio over its steam predecessor, pioneers like Whitehead and the Wrights were thus able to improve upon the ground-breaking work of John Stringfellow from over half a century earlier. As Sir Isaac Newton succinctly put it in 1675: "If I have seen further it is by standing on the shoulders of giants."

And so, in answer to the above question, while Gustave Whitehead and the Wright brothers rightly deserve their places in aviation history, it is actually to a man from an earlier time that the accolade must go. I give you John Stringfellow, the Father of Powered Flight!

FORTY

SIR DAVID ATTENBOROUGH AND THE BARNES BRIDGE MYSTERY

Kate Webster liked to drink, and the place where she most enjoyed quenching her thirst was a public house in the London suburb of Richmond, called the 'Hole in the Wall'. Unmarried, and with a young son, Kate was 30 years old and in need of work. Julia Martha Thomas was a retired schoolteacher who lived at 2 Mayfield Cottages, Park Road, Richmond, and she was on the lookout for someone to help with domestic duties around the house. So it was that, in January 1879, Julia employed Kate in the capacity of housemaid.

Unfortunately, it soon became apparent that Kate's somewhat lax approach to her duties fell well short of Julia's exacting standards. After just one month, Julia decided to dispense with Kate's services and duly gave her notice to leave.

Barnes Railway Bridge

On 5 March 1879, a coal porter discovered a large trunk on the shore of the River Thames, close to the Barnes Railway Bridge. To his horror, on opening the chest he discovered that it contained the body of a woman, minus the head and one foot. While the missing foot was soon found in nearby Twickenham, the head remained unaccounted for, and as a consequence identification of the deceased was likely to prove extremely problematic, given the rudimentary forensic techniques available to late-nineteenth-century investigators. The discovery of the remains of the unidentified woman drew the immediate interest of the local press, who were quick to label the case the 'Barnes Mystery'.

It was not long, however, before neighbours of Julia Thomas became concerned that she had not been seen coming and going for a number of weeks. In addition, Kate Webster, who was known to own little of value, suddenly seemed to be in possession of a significant amount of household furnishings, which she was in the process of trying to sell.

Kate Webster

The police were notified and immediately carried out a search of 2 Mayfield Cottages. The scene that greeted the investigating officers was not a pleasant one. Bloodstains were found almost everywhere, charred bones littered the grate of the fire, and a fatty substance was discovered behind the laundry boiler. An attempt had been made to clean up some of the bloodstains, with only limited success. The body in the trunk and the missing householder were deemed to be one and the same, and Kate Webster was subsequently arrested and charged with murder. Her trial began on 2 July 1879.

Throughout the proceedings, Webster tried to apportion blame for the killing on to others, although each of those she accused had alibis that effectively cleared them of any wrongdoing. Kate Webster was eventually convicted of the murder of Julia Thomas and, as was standard practice at the time, was sentenced to be hanged. On the eve of her execution, Kate eventually confessed, to a priest, that she alone had committed the crime.

She went on to explain that the pair had argued on Julia's return home from church and that, in the ensuing struggle, Kate had thrown her employer from the top of the stairs to the ground floor. Concerned that neighbours would be alerted by her screams, Kate next grabbed Julia by the throat in an effort to silence her. Tragically, her efforts were all too successful, and Julia was silenced forever.

In an attempt to dispose of the body, Kate had removed the head and limbs, boiling some of them in the laundry tub and burning others in the fireplace. Most of the remains she had put in the trunk that was found near Barnes Railway Bridge, and what she couldn't fit in the trunk she removed from the house in a bag. For reasons that were not entirely clear, she chose not to reveal where she had disposed of the victim's head. Kate Webster, who was executed at Wandsworth Jail on 29 July 1879, must have thought she had taken that secret to her grave.

A contemporary depiction of the execution of Kate Webster

The mortal remains of Julia Thomas that had been recovered were laid to rest in an unmarked plot in Barnes Cemetery.

All very interesting, you may be thinking, *but what the Dickens has all this got to do with the renowned broadcaster and naturalist, Sir David Attenborough?* Well, I was just coming to that. Remember the pub where Kate used to like to go to get sozzled? Yes, that's right: the Hole in the Wall. Well, that pub just happens to be next door to Sir David's house, and in 2009, after it closed its doors for the last time, he bought the pub in order to save it from being sold to a property developer. During work to convert the former hostelry into an extension to Sir David's home, contractors unearthed a human skull!

The skull was missing its teeth, and fracture marks suggested that the individual had suffered some kind of trauma, possibly occasioned by a fall downstairs. Additionally, the skull contained unusually low

Scenes of crime: the cottage where the murder took place is on the left, Sir David's house is in the centre behind some trees, and the former Hole in the Wall pub is on the right

collagen levels, indicating that it may have been boiled! In the opinion of the local coroner, there was "clear, convincing and compelling evidence" that the skull belonged to Julia Martha Thomas.

Unfortunately for Julia, details of the exact location in Barnes Cemetery where the rest of her remains had been interred had, in the intervening years, been lost, and consequently it wasn't possible to reunite her head and body. Nevertheless, it is thanks to the unwitting intervention of one of the world's most respected broadcasters that the last remaining puzzle of the Barnes Bridge Mystery was finally solved. Well done, Sir David!

FORTY-ONE

WANTED, DEAD AND ALIVE

As bandits go, the name of Elmer McCurdy may not be up there with the likes of Jesse James or Butch Cassidy, but for sheer incompetence he stands alone. His life of crime was littered with bungled attempted robberies that were so inept they have become the stuff of legend.

Born on 1 January 1880 to Sadie McCurdy, an unmarried 17-year-old, Elmer was adopted by Sadie's brother and sister-in-law in order to stave off the stigma of illegitimacy. As a young adult, McCurdy trained as a plumber, a job he seemed suited to until he was made redundant due to an economic recession in 1898. Shortly thereafter, he began to lead an itinerant lifestyle, drifting from place to place, drinking heavily and working only occasionally.

In 1907, Elmer elected to join the United States Army, where he was trained to use nitro-glycerine:

a highly explosive liquid for demolition purposes. Discharged from the army in 1910, McCurdy made the fateful decision to use his new-found pyrotechnic skills for criminal purposes. Unfortunately, as will soon become apparent, Elmer does not appear to have been the most attentive of pupils.

Elmer McCurdy

Hearing that the Iron Mountain–Missouri Pacific Railroad was carrying a safe containing 4,000 dollars, he decided to try his hand at train robbery. Managing to stop the train and locate the safe, McCurdy became somewhat over-zealous in his application of nitro-glycerine to the safe door. Instead of just removing the door, the blast destroyed the entire safe and most of its contents. Charred remnants of bank notes fluttered about the carriage and most of the silver coins had been fused to the safe walls by the explosion. In total, Elmer and his cronies only managed to steal about 450 dollars between them.

McCurdy's next target was the Citizens Bank in Chautauqua, Kansas, which was treated to his unique style of banditry in September 1911. Having spent two hours hammering his way through the bank wall, he again overdid it with the nitro-glycerine charge and blew the door of the bank's vault right through the inside of the building, destroying everything in its path but without damaging the safe inside. Elmer next tried to blow open the safe, but this time the charge failed to explode. Having by now made enough noise to waken the dead, the hopeless desperados were forced to flee with just 150 dollars in coins that had been left in a tray outside the safe.

In October 1911, McCurdy heard on the grapevine that a train carrying a massive 400,000 dollars in cash would shortly be passing through Okesa, Oklahoma. Of course, Elmer held up the wrong train, and he left with a paltry 46 dollars and a couple of bottles of whisky that he had managed to coax out of the startled passengers. A contemporary newspaper account of the hold-up referred to it as "one of the smallest in the history of train robbery".

Nevertheless, McCurdy was by now a wanted man, and a 2,000-dollar reward was offered for his capture. On the morning of 7 October, a posse of sheriffs with bloodhounds tracked Elmer to a hay shed, where he had been hiding out while consuming the stolen whisky. Elmer McCurdy was killed by a single shot to the chest, inflicted upon him while he was lying down, presumably incapacitated by drink. The reward paid to the sheriffs exceeded the amount that McCurdy had managed to steal during his entire criminal career by a factor of three!

However, it is not for what he failed to achieve in life that McCurdy is best remembered today. Bizarrely, Elmer's career only really took off once he was dead! His corpse was delivered to the Johnson Funeral Home in Pawhuska, Oklahoma, where the undertaker, Joseph Johnson, awaited the arrival of next-of-kin to make arrangements for the burial. However, as the days passed and the body remained unclaimed, Johnson decided to embalm Elmer with an arsenic-based preservative that would effectively mummify the remains until such time as a living relative could be found.

Unfortunately, as time went on, and with nobody coming forward to claim the mortal remains of Elmer

McCurdy, the undertaker grew impatient and wanted to be paid for his services. It was at this point that the entrepreneurial corpse-minder hit upon the idea of putting Elmer on display and charging visitors a nickel to see 'The Bandit Who Wouldn't Give Up'. He dressed McCurdy in street clothes and stood him up in the corner of the funeral home, rifle in hand! Elmer was an immediate hit, and Johnson received several offers for the mummy, but he refused all approaches because his dead companion was proving to be very lucrative indeed.

Elmer in his coffin

Joseph Johnson's money-making scheme came to an end on 6 October 1916, when a man claiming to be Elmer's long-lost brother came forward to claim the remains. Johnson reluctantly released the body to him, although the 'relative' turned out to be the owner of a travelling carnival who promptly put McCurdy on display, billing him as 'the outlaw who would never be captured alive'. Elmer McCurdy continued to prove a popular attraction for the next three decades, until the owner of the carnival died in 1949, whereupon the macabre exhibit was placed in storage in a warehouse in Los Angeles.

Elmer was not entirely forgotten, though. In 1967, he made an appearance in the film *She Freak*, and in 1968 he was exhibited at a show at Mount Rushmore. Subsequently, the remains were sold to the owner of an amusement park in Long Beach, California, where the dehydrated outlaw remained, hanging from gallows, until 1976, when a shocked worker realised that the mannequin he had been asked to move was actually a human corpse.

The Los Angeles Coroner's Office conducted an investigation and was eventually able to identify the remains as being those of McCurdy. On 22 April 1977, Elmer McCurdy was finally laid to rest at the Summit View Cemetery in Guthrie, Oklahoma, more than 65 years after his death. Around 300 people attended the graveside service – quite a turnout for a man who no one wanted to bury!

IMAGES

Gustave Whitehead This media file is in the **public domain** *in the* USA.

Gustave Whitehead's 'Number 21' Valerian Gribayedoff (1858–1908). This work is in the **public domain** in its country of origin and other countries and areas where the copyright term is the author's **life plus 100 years or less**.

The Wright brothers' 'Flyer' John T. Daniels, 17 December 1903. This media file is in the **public domain** *in the* USA. This applies to US works where the copyright has expired, often because its first publication *occurred prior to 1 January 1923*.

G. K. Chesterton Unknown, 1914. This media file is in the **public domain** *in the* USA. This applies to US works where the copyright has expired, often because its first publication *occurred prior to 1 January 1923*.

Interesting company logo Unknown, 1852. Great Seal of the London Necropolis and National Mausoleum Company. This UK artistic work, of which the author is **unknown** and cannot be ascertained by reasonable enquiry, is in the **public domain**.

The damaged terminus of the London Necropolis Company Southern Railway Photographic Unit (British Railways Board after 1948) 16-17 April 1941. Aftermath of the bombing of the London Necropolis Railway's buildings in London, night of April 16-17, 1941. This work created by the UK Government *is in the* **public domain**.

Gregor MacGregor (1786–1845) Martín Tovar y Tovar (1827–1902). General Gregorio MacGregor 1874. This work is in the **public domain** in its country of origin and other countries and areas where the copyright term is the author's **life plus 100 years or less**.

Francisco de Miranda (1750–1816) Martin Tovar y Tovar, 1874. This work is in the **public domain** in its country of origin and other countries and areas where the copyright term is the author's **life plus 70 years or less**.

Simon Bolivar (1783–1830) Arturo Michelena (1863–1898). Galería de Arte Nacional. This work was first published in Venezuela *and is now in the* **public domain** *because its copyright protection has expired.* This media file is in the **public domain** *in the* USA.

Poyais, as depicted in MacGregor's guidebook Thomas Strangeways (pseudonym). Engraving from 'Sketch of the Mosquito Shore' purporting to depict the Port of Black River in the non-existent Territory of Poyais. 1822. This work is in the **public domain** in its country of origin and other countries and areas where the copyright term is the author's **life plus 70 years or less**. This work is in the **public domain** in the USA because it was published (or registered with the US Copyright Office) before 1 January 1923.

A Bank of Poyais dollar note Godot13. **National Numismatic Collection, National Museum of American History at the Smithsonian Institution.** This work is in the **public domain** in the USA because it was published (or registered with the US Copyright Office) before 1 January 1923.

Amerigo Vespucci (1454–1512) "Amerigo Vespucci, nobile fiorentino discopritore dell'America." by B. J. Lossing (1813–1891) is licensed under CC0 1.0.

John Cabot (c.1450–c.1500) "John Cabot and his three sons from the picture in the Palace of the Doges, Venice." by B. J. Lossing, (1813–1891) is licensed under CC0 1.0.

Sir Edmund Godfrey Unknown, 17th century. Sir Edmund Berry Godfrey. This work is in the **public domain** in its country of origin and other countries and areas where the copyright term is the author's **life plus 70 years or less.**

Titus Oates (1649–1705) "Titus Oates" by *Skara kommun* is licensed under CC BY 2.0.

A later depiction of King Arthur and Excalibur Howard Pyle illustration from the 1903 edition of *The Story of King Arthur and His Knights.* This work is in the **public domain** in its country of origin and other countries and areas where the copyright term is the author's **life plus 100 years or less.** This work is in the **public domain** in the USA because it was published (or registered with the US Copyright Office) before 1 January 1923.

An enigmatic artefact if ever there was one! Superchilum 4 May 2014. This file is licensed under the Creative Commons Attribution-Share Alike 4.0 International licence.

Sarah Winchester in 1865 Taber Photographic Co., 1865. This work is in the **public domain** in its country of origin and other countries and areas where the copyright term is the author's **life plus 70 years or less.**

Winchester House "Winchester Mystery House" by *Julie Markee* is licensed under CC BY 2.0.

Dan Donnelly Drawn by George Sharples; engraved by Percy Roberts. This work is in the **public domain** in its country of origin and other countries and areas where the copyright term is the author's **life plus 100 years or less.**

The CS Mackay-Bennett Unknown, c.1884. Le Site du Titanic.

RMS Titanic "RMS *Titanic*" by *Cliff* is licensed under CC BY 2.0.

John Jacob Astor IV "John Jacob Astor IV (1864-1912)" by Bonnat, Léon Joseph Florentin, (1833–1922) is licensed under CC0 1.0.

Paracelsus (1493–1541) "2009-11-15 München, Alte Pinakothek 098 Peter Paul Rubens, Portrait von Paracelsus" by *Allie Caulfield* is licensed under CC BY 2.0.

A nineteenth-century illustration of Cock Lane Unknown. Original sketch found in: C. Mackay (1852), *Haunted Houses*.

A nineteenth-century illustration of the haunted room Original sketch found in: C. Mackay (1852), *Haunted Houses*. Grant, D., *The Cock Lane Ghost* (page 7) declares it to be "J. W. Archer".

Cock Lane in the twenty-first century Iridescent. 11 August 2009.

Ouch! "Mrs Holland avocado" by Malcolm Manners is licensed under CC BY 2.0.

A sabot maker "Henry Ossawa Tanner & quot; The Young Sabot Maker & quot; 1895 (detail)" by *Plum leaves* is licensed under CC BY 2.0

Julius Caesar "Portret van Julius Caesar, Andries Vaillant (1665–1693)" by Andries Vaillant is licensed under CC0 1.0.

An example of a velocipede "Velocipede" by Bill Ward is licensed under CC BY 2.0.

Jean-Pierre Blanchard This work is in the **public domain** in its country of origin and other countries and areas where the copyright term is the author's **life plus 100 years or less**.

Blanchard and Jeffries head out over the water "LTA, Balloons, France, Jean-Pierre Blanchard, Channel flight

(1785) with Jeffries" by Public.Resource.Org is licensed under CC BY 2.0.

Bill Coltman Unknown, 1918.

Domestic disharmony "Frederick Hendrik Kaemmerer – The Argument" by *Irina* is licensed under CC BY 2.0.

A wife auction in progress Unknown, 1820.

Thomas Hardy Bain News Service, publisher, between c.1910 and c.1915.

Hermann Goering Bundesarchiv, Bild 102-15607 / CC-BY-SA 3.0

The body of Hermann Goering This image is the work of a US Army *soldier or employee, taken or made as part of that person's official duties. As a* work *of the* US federal government, the image is in the **public domain.**

The caves in which the scrolls were found "Caves@Dead Sea Scrolls" by Lux Moundi is licensed under CC BY 2.0.

A section of the copper scroll This work is in the **public domain** in its country of origin and other countries and areas where the copyright term is the author's **life plus 70 years or less.**

Mark Twain, sporting his trademark moustache Mathew Brady. Photographed 7 February 1871. This work is in the **public domain** in its country of origin and other countries and areas where the copyright term is the author's **life plus 100 years or less.**

In his later years Photographer: A. F. Bradley. In his studio, 1907. This media file is in the **public domain** *in the* USA. This applies to US works where the copyright has expired, often because its first publication *occurred prior to 1 January 1923.*

Reverend George Gilfillan (1813–1878). In addition to his ministerial duties, Gilfillan was also a poet in his own right G. J. Stodart (Engraver). (Lifetime: died 1884). 1878. This work is in the **public domain** in the USA because it was published (or registered with the US Copyright Office) before 1 January 1923.

Larry Foley (1847–1917) Unknown, before 1917. This image was created in Australia and is now classified as being in the **public domain** *because its term of copyright has now expired.*

Wilfrid Voynich (1865–1930) Unknown, 1900. This work is in the **public domain** in its country of origin and other countries and areas where the copyright term is the author's **life plus 70 years or less**.

Athanasius Kircher (1602–1680) "Kircher, Athanasius" by Janssonius, Johannes d. J. & Elizeus Weyerstraten is licensed under PDM 1.0.

Photograph of a section of the Voynich Manuscript "Voynich" by D. C. Atty is licensed under CC BY 2.0.

The skull with hair still attached to the forehead Unknown, ca 1941. This work is in the **public domain.**

Mysterious graffiti David Buttery (Loganberry (Talk) May 2006). I, the copyright holder of this work, release this work into the **public domain**. This applies worldwide.

Maria and Wolfgang with their father "Wolfgang Amadeus Mozart with his sister Maria Anna and father Leopold. On the wall a portrait of his dead mother Anna Maria, by Johann Nepomuk della Croce. ca 1780" by Royal Opera House Covent Garden is licensed under CC BY 2.0.

Katharine Wright This image is in the **public domain** in the USA.

Wilhelmina, before the onset of mental illness Unknown, c.1880. This work is in the **public domain** in its country of origin and other countries and areas where the copyright term is the author's **life plus 70 years or less**.

Ama Jetsun Pema VOA, 22 April 2009. This media is in the **public domain** in the USA because it solely consists of material created and provided by **Voice of America**, the official external broadcasting service of the federal government of the USA.

Babe Ruth in action Charles M. Conlon, 1916. This media file is in the **public domain** *in the* USA.

Woolly mammoth Flying Puffin, 1 July 2011. This file is licensed under the Creative Commons Attribution-Share Alike 2.0 Generic licence.

Pyramid of Djoser "Saqqara, step pyramid of Djoser" by Arian Zwegers is licensed under CC BY 2.0.

Jack the Ripper? John Tenniel, published 29 September 1888. The author died in 1914, so this work is in the **public domain** in its country of origin and other countries and areas where the copyright term is the author's **life plus 100 years or less**.

The guillotine "A Guillotine" by *alex.ch* is licensed under CC BY 2.0.

Early depictions of the face of Jesus "Portrait of Christ" by Byzantine via the Metropolitan Museum of Art is licensed under CC0 1.0. "Cameo with Christ Emmanuel" by Byzantine via the Metropolitan Museum of Art is licensed under CC0 1.0.

Veil of Veronica, St Peter's Basilica This image is in the **public domain** in the USA.

The Manoppello Image Image: http://www.voltosanto. it/ This work is in the **public domain** in its country of origin and other countries and areas where the copyright term is the author's **life plus 70 years or less**.

Pope Benedict XVI Peter Nguyen, 6 July 2011. CC-BY This file is licensed under the Creative Commons Attribution 2.0 Generic licence.

Gerhard Weinberg in 2006 Lllmmmnnn 25 April 2006. This work is licensed under the Creative Commons Attribution-Share Alike 3.0 *Licen*ce.

Adolf Hitler (1889–1945) Attribution: Bundesarchiv, Bild 183-S33882 / CC-BY-SA 3.0. This file is licensed under the Creative Commons Attribution-Share Alike 3.0 Germany licence.

King Charles I (1600–1649) "Charles I, Daniel Mytens". Charles I, King of England, 1600-1649 is licensed under CC0 1.0.

John Bigg (1629–1696) http://wellcomeimages. org/indexplus/obf_images/50/2a/ a229f5036664c956cf4f386126ba.jpg This file is licensed under the Creative Commons Attribution 4.0 International licence.

Sir Edmund Hillary and Sherpa Tenzing Norgay Jamling Tenzing Norgay, 29 May 1953. This file is licensed under the Creative Commons Attribution-Share Alike 3.0 Unported, 2.5 Generic, 2.0 Generic and 1.0 Generic licence.

George Mallory Alexander Frederick Richmond Wollaston, 1921. This work is in the **public domain** in its country of origin and other countries and areas where the copyright term is the author's **life plus 70 years or less.**

Andrew 'Sandy' Irvine Unknown, c.1920. This work is in the **public domain** in its country of origin and other countries and areas where the copyright term is the author's **life plus 70 years or less.**

Young Agatha This work is in the **public domain** *in the* USA because it was published *in the* USA between 1923 and 1977 **without a copyright notice.**

Archibald Christie This work is in the **public domain** in its country of origin and other countries and areas where the copyright term is the author's **life plus 70 years or less.**

Agatha's disappearance made headlines on both sides of the Atlantic This work is in the **public domain** in its country of origin and other countries and areas where the copyright term is the author's **life plus 70 years or less.**

Max and Agatha Unknown, 12 May 2014. This image is in the **public domain** because the copyright of this photograph, registered in Argentina, has expired.

Bletchley Park, home of the codebreakers "Bletchley Park" by *Draco2008* is licensed under CC BY 2.0.

The Pig War Thomas Nast, 28 April 1877. This media file is in the **public domain** *in the* USA.

King Alfonso XII of Spain This work is in the **public domain** in its country of origin and other countries and areas where the copyright term is the author's **life plus 70 years or less.**

Oliver Cromwell (1599–1658) This work is in the **public domain** in its country of origin and other countries and areas where the copyright term is the author's **life plus 100 years or less.**

John Hampden (ca 1595–1643) This work is in the **public domain** in its country of origin and other countries and areas where the copyright term is the author's **life plus 100 years or less.**

King Charles I (1600–1649) This work is in the **public domain** in its country of origin and other countries and areas where the copyright term is the author's **life plus 100 years or less.**

Statue of John Hampden in Aylesbury, Buckinghamshire D. Gore. 1994 This file is licensed under the Creative Commons Attribution-Share Alike 2.0 Generic licence.

King John "King John" by R. Sheppard (fl. 1730–1740) is licensed under CC0 1.0.

Edward I "Eduardus II Rex Aug." Edward I, King of England, 1239–1307 is licensed under CC0 1.0.

Anne Boleyn This work is in the **public domain** in its country of origin and other countries and areas where the copyright term is the author's **life plus 100 years or less.**

Edward VI (1537–1553) "Edward VI (1537–1553), when Duke of Cornwall" by Workshop of Hans Holbein the Younger via The Metropolitan Museum of Art is licensed under CC0 1.0.

King Charles I (1600–1649) This work is in the **public domain** in its country of origin and other countries and areas where the copyright term is the author's **life plus 100 years or less.**

Cora Crippen This work is from the George Grantham Bain *collection at the* Library of Congress. According to the library, there are no known copyright restrictions *on the use of this work.*

Hawley Harvey Crippen Hawley Harvey Crippen. Originally published in 1910. Copyright expired. This media file is in the **public domain** *in the* USA. This applies to US works where the copyright has expired, often because its first publication *occurred prior to 1 January 1923.*

Dr Crippen and Ethel Le Neve at a remand hearing Dr Crippen and Ethel Le Neve on trial, London. This work is from the George Grantham Bain *collection at the* Library of Congress. According to the library, there are no known copyright restrictions *on the use of this work.*

An artist's impression of the Aerial 1843. This work is in the **public domain** in its country of origin and other countries and areas where the copyright term is the author's **life plus 70 years or less.**

John Stringfellow This work is in the **public domain** in its country of origin and other countries and areas where the copyright term is the author's **life plus 70 years or less.**

William Samuel Henson Before 1888. This work is in the **public domain** in its country of origin and other countries and areas where the copyright term is the author's **life plus 70 years or less.**

Stringfellow's flying machine Picture taken at the Science Museum, London, 2 January 2006. No machine-readable author provided. Gaius Cornelius assumed (based on copyright claims). I, the copyright holder of this work, release this work into the **public domain.** This applies worldwide. I grant anyone the right to use this work **for any purpose,** without any conditions, unless such conditions are required by law.

Barnes Railway Bridge Sunil060902. Barnes Bridge looking west from south bank of the Thames. This file is licensed under the Creative Commons Attribution-Share Alike 3.0 Unported licence.

Appendix 2

SOURCES

Wright? Wrong!
gustave-whitehead.com
https://en.wikipedia.org/wiki/Gustave_Whitehead

The Train Now Departing
http://www.planetslade.com/necropolis-railway1.html
https://en.wikipedia.org/wiki/London_Necropolis_Railway

The Prince of Poyais
http://www.toptenz.net/top-10-true-stories-movies.php
https://en.wikipedia.org/wiki/Gregor_MacGregor
*https://www.measuringworth.com/ukcompare/relativevalue.
php*

America – Amerigo or Amerike?
*http://www.bbc.co.uk/history/british/tudors/americaname_01.
shtml*
https://en.wikipedia.org/wiki/Amerigo_Vespucci
https://en.wikipedia.org/wiki/Richard_Amerike

Who Killed Sir Edmund Godfrey?

https://esoterx.com/2015/02/18/puns-kill-the-murder-of-sir-edmund-berry-godfrey/

http://weirdthingshappenalltime.blogspot.co.uk/2007/11/mystery-of-greenberry-hill-sir-edmond.html

Was King Arthur Part Italian?

http://www.ancient-origins.net/artifacts-other-artifacts/legendary-sword-stone-san-galgano-002968

https://www.theguardian.com/world/2001/sep/16/rorycarroll.theobserver

The House That Sarah Built

https://www.prairieghosts.com/winchester.html

https://en.wikipedia.org/wiki/Sarah_Winchester

Dan Donnelly's Arm

https://en.wikipedia.org/wiki/Dan_Donnelly_(boxer)

http://www.theboxingglove.com/2015/03/the-legend-of-dan-donnelly-irelands.html

The Unknown Child

https://en.wikipedia.org/wiki/CS_Mackay-Bennett

https://uk.pinterest.com/pin/388224430350007190/

The Memory of Water

* The Statistics Portal

Scratching Fanny: The Cock Lane Ghost

Ashford, J. (2017). 'The Unseen Hand'. BleedRed Books and CreateSpace.

http://www.walksoflondon.co.uk/35/true-ghost-stories-the-co.shtml

inflation.stephenmorley.org

https://en.wikipedia.org/wiki/Cock_Lane

The Surprising History of Everyday Words

https://www.phactual.com/the-unexpected-history-of-words-we-all-know/

http://www.todayifoundout.com/index.php/2012/05/avocado-derives-from-a-word-meaning-testicle/

http://mentalfloss.com/article/50179/how-did-caesarean-sections-get-their-name

http://list25.com/25-interesting-and-somewhat-strange-word-origins/

The Rise and Fall of Jean-Pierre Blanchard

https://lflank.wordpress.com/2017/05/23/blanchards-cross-channel-balloon-flight/#more-1391d

https://en.wikipedia.org/wiki/Jean-Pierre_Blanchard

https://www.britannica.com/biography/Jean-Pierre-Francois-Blanchard

https://en.wikipedia.org/wiki/Montgolfier_brothers

The Remarkable War of Lance Corporal William Harold Coltman

http://www.abroadintheyard.com/britains-most-decorated-enlisted-soldier-ww1-conscientious-objector/

https://en.wikipedia.org/wiki/William_Coltman

https://en.wikipedia.org/wiki/Croix_de_Guerre

Till Cash Us Do Part

http://www.todayifoundout.com/index.php/2016/11/surprisingly-recent-time-british-history-husbands-sold-wives-market/

https://en.wikipedia.org/wiki/Wife_selling_(English_custom)

The Nice Herr Goering

http://www.auschwitz.dk/albert.htm

https://en.wikipedia.org/wiki/Hermann_Goring

The Copper Scroll Treasure
http://www.ancient-origins.net/ancient-places-asia/lost-treasure-copper-scroll-001457
https://en.wikipedia.org/wiki/Dead_Sea_Scrolls

Mark Twain: Hero of the American Civil War?
http://www.abroadintheyard.com/
https://en.wikipedia.org/wiki/Mark_Twain
http://www.cmgww.com/historic/twain/about/bio.htm

The World's Worst Poet
http://www.mcgonagall-online.org.uk/
https://en.wikipedia.org/wiki/William_McGonagall

Lord Loincloth and the Rumble in the Jungle
https://lflank.wordpress.com/2017/10/04/tanganyika-the-naval-battle-in-the-jungle
https://en.wikipedia.org/wiki/Geoffrey_Spicer-Simson
https://en.wikipedia.org/wiki/Lake_Tanganyika
https://en.wikipedia.org/wiki/MV_Liemba

The Phantom Doggie of Logierait Parish
https://esoterx.com/2017/10/31/friends-dont-let-friends-hunt-ghosts-the-dogged-haunting-of-ballechin-house/
http://dark-stories.com/eng/the_ballechin_house.htm
https://www.wikitree.com/wiki/Steuart-69

Was Lord Haw-Haw a Traitor?
http://mysteryinthehistory.com/who-was-lord-haw-haw/
https://en.wikipedia.org/wiki/William_Joyce

Gordon Bennett, it's Sweet Fanny Adams!
http://www.phrases.org.uk/
https://en.wikipedia.org/wiki/John_Thomas_and_Lady_Jane

The Voynich Manuscript

voynich.nu
https://en.wikipedia.org/wiki/Wilfrid_Voynich

Who Put Bella in the Wych Elm?

http://www.independent.co.uk/news/uk/home-news/is-this-the-bella-in-the-wych-elm-unravelling-the-mystery-of-the-skull-found-in-a-tree-trunk-8546497.html
http://theunredacted.com/the-hagley-woods-mystery-bella-in-the-wych-elm/
https://en.wikipedia.org/wiki/Who_put_Bella_in_the_Wych_Elm%3F

Oh, Sister!

http://listverse.com/2016/12/13/10-surprising-sisters-of-famous-historical-figures/
https://en.wikipedia.org/wiki/Maria_Anna_Mozart
http://worldofpoe.blogspot.co.uk/2009/11/strange-case-of-rosalie-poe.html
http://www.irishidentity.com/extras/gaels/stories/wilde.html

What's That Doing There?

http://www.ancient-wisdom.com/ooparts.htm
* geology.about.com

Strange but True!

http://kottke.org/14/02/unlikely-simultaneous-historical-events
http://io9.gizmodo.com/5896262/the-last-mammoths-died-out-just-3600-years-agobut-they-should-have-survived
http://www.history.com/this-day-in-history/a-thousand-pioneers-head-west-on-the-oregon-trail
https://en.wikipedia.org

The Veil of Veronica

https://www.gotquestions.org/Jesus-of-Nazareth.html

http://www.newworldencyclopedia.org/entry/Veil_of_Veronica
https://www.catholicculture.org/culture/library/view.
cfm?recnum=6346
http://www.catholicnewsagency.com/news/an-encounter-
with-the-manoppello-image-of-the-face-of-christ-95030/

Hitler's Second Book
http://www.telegraph.co.uk/culture/books/3603289/Revealed-
the-amazing-story-behind-Hitlers-second-book.html
https://en.wikipedia.org/wiki/Zweites_Buch

Misadventures in Tudor England
darwinawards.com
tudoraccidents.history.ox.ac.uk

The Regicidal Hermit
https://en.wikipedia.org/wiki/Dinton,_Buckinghamshire
http://www.eyewitnesstohistory.com/charlesI.htm

On Top of the World
http://biography.yourdictionary.com/george-mallory
http://www.telegraph.co.uk/news/worldnews/
australiaandthepacific/australia/7735660/Who-really-
was-first-to-climb-Mount-Everest.html
http://garethdthomas.homestead.com/malloryandirvine.html

The Mystery of Christie
http://mentalfloss.com/article/52724/11-reasons-agatha-
christie-was-interesting-her-characters
https://en.wikipedia.org/wiki/Agatha_Christie

The World's Weirdest Wars
unrealfacts.com/stupidest-wars-history-ever/

John Hampden: Father of Democracy?
http://bcw-project.org/biography/john-hampden

https://en.wikipedia.org/wiki/John_Hampden

*http://www.parliament.uk/about/mps-and-lords/principal/
black-rod/*

Rest in Peace?

*http://www.abroadintheyard.com/corpses-kings-queens-
england-exhumed/*

The Disappearance of Cora Crippen

*http://www.historytoday.com/richard-cavendish/execution-dr-
crippen*

http://www.bbc.co.uk/news/magazine-10802059

https://en.wikipedia.org/wiki/Hawley_Harvey_Crippen

John Stringfellow: The Father of Powered Flight

http://www.chardmuseum.co.uk/powered-flight/

https://en.wikipedia.org/wiki/Aerial_steam_carriage

Sir David Attenborough and the Barnes Bridge Mystery

*http://mentalfloss.com/article/505155/barnes-mystery-
twisted-tale-maids-murder-and-mistaken-identity*

*https://en.wikipedia.org/wiki/Murder_of_Julia_Martha_
Thomas*

Wanted, Dead and Alive

*https://the-line-up.com/5-very-creepy-happenings-history-
never-heard*

https://en.wikipedia.org/wiki/Elmer_McCurdy

CPSIA information can be obtained
at www.ICGtesting.com
Printed in the USA
FSHW010501070619
58835FS